The Nature of Economic Growth

Other Books by the Author

Growth and Development: with Special Reference to
    Developing Economies (Sixth Edition)
Inflation, Saving and Growth in Developing Economies
Regional Growth and Unemployment in the United Kingdom
    (*with R. Dixon*)
Financing Economic Development
Balance-of-Payments Theory and the United Kingdom
    Experience (Fourth Edition *with H. Gibson*)
Nicholas Kaldor
UK Industrialisation and Deindustrialisation (Third Edition
    with S. Bazen)
The Performance and Prospects of the Pacific Island
    Economies in the World Economy
Economic Growth and the Balance-of-Payments Constraint
    (*with J. McCombie*)
The Economics of Growth and Development: Selected
    Essays, Vol. 1
Macroeconomic Issues from a Keynesian Perspective:
    Selected Essays, Vol. 2

Edited Works

Keynes and International Monetary Relations
Keynes and Laissez-Faire
Keynes and the Bloomsbury Group (*with D. Crabtree*)
Keynes as a Policy Adviser
Keynes and Economic Development
Keynes and the Role of the State (*with D. Crabtree*)
European Factor Mobility: Trends and Consequences
    (*with I. Gordon*)
The Essential Kaldor (*with F. Targetti*)
Further Essays in Economic Theory and Policy, Volume
    9, Collected Economic Papers of N. Kaldor (*with F.
    Targetti*)
Causes of Growth and Stagnation in the World Economy
    (the Mattioli Lectures of N. Kaldor *with F. Targetti*)
Economic Dynamics, Trade and Growth: Essays on Harrodian
    Themes (*with G. Rampa and L. Stella*)

The Nature of Economic Growth

An Alternative Framework for Understanding the Performance of Nations

A.P. Thirlwall

Professor of Applied Economics, University of Kent at Canterbury, UK

Edward Elgar
Cheltenham, UK • Northampton, MA, USA

Published by
Edward Elgar Publishing Limited
Glensanda House
Montpellier Parade
Cheltenham
Glos GL50 1UA
UK

Edward Elgar Publishing, Inc.
William Pratt House
9 Dewey Court
Northampton
Massachusetts 01060
USA

This book has been printed on demand to keep the title in print.

A catalogue record for this book is available from the British Library

Library of Congress Cataloguing in Publication Data
Thirlwall, A. P.
    The nature of economic growth : an alternative framework for understanding the performance of nations / A.P. Thirlwall.
        p. cm.
    Includes index.
        1. Economic development. I. Title.

HD82 .T483 2002
338.9—dc21

2001051074

ISBN 978 1 84064 864 5 (cased)
ISBN 978 1 84376 338 3 (paperback)

Contents

To my Grandchildren,
Lorenzo and Sienna

Preface

This short book has arisen out of a series of lectures and seminars that I gave at the National University of Mexico in September 2000. They, in turn, were based on a selection of lectures I have been giving for a long time at the University of Kent to students studying for a Master's degree in development economics. The fact that the lectures were given to graduate students, however, does not mean that the book will not be intelligible to others, including undergraduates and practitioners in the development field. First of all, the basic principles of growth and development theory are not that difficult to grasp by anyone with a willingness and interest to learn, and secondly, following the dictum of Alfred Marshall (the great 19th-century Cambridge economist), I have tried to translate theoretical models expressed in mathematics into words.

The matter of why some countries are rich and others are poor, and why some countries grow faster than others over long periods of time (although not necessarily continuously), has always fascinated me as an economist, and in the chapters to follow I try to present the conventional wisdom, as it has evolved historically, but with a critical eye, from Adam Smith, the author of *An Inquiry into the Nature and Causes of the Wealth of Nations* (1776) to 'new' or endogenous growth theory. I am critical of the latter, and its predecessor, neoclassical growth theory, and my own contribution is to try and put (back) demand into growth theory as a driving force. In my view, neoclassical and 'new' growth theory is far too supply-oriented in its approach, not recognizing sufficiently the various constraints on demand long before supply constraints bite. In an open, developing economy one of the major constraints is the availability of foreign exchange to pay for imports, so that export growth which relaxes a balance of payments constraint on demand becomes a crucial determinant of overall growth performance. This is entirely missing from 'new' growth theory, but is a central feature of my own thinking and research. There are not many developing countries in the world that could not utilize resources more fully, and grow faster, given greater availability of foreign exchange. Within this framework, the main factors of production – labour and capital – are considered to be elastic to demand, and so too is productivity growth based on static and dynamic returns to scale, captured by Verdoorn's Law. Demand creating its own supply (within limits) in a growth context (as well as in a static context), rather than the pre-Keynesian view of supply creating its own demand, provides an alternative framework to the neoclassical one for understanding the differential growth perform-ance of nations.

I am grateful to Dr Roberto Escalante (Chairman of the Department), and his colleagues at the National University of Mexico, for the opportunity to give these lectures, and to write this short book, and for the feedback on them.

I am also grateful to the editor of *Banca Nazionale del Lavoro Quarterly Review* for allowing me to reproduce in Chapter 6 certain material published in the December 2000 issue of the journal.

A.P.T.

1. Growth theory in the history of thought

Growth and development theory is at least as old as Adam Smith's famous book published in 1776 entitled *An Inquiry into the Nature and Causes of the Wealth of Nations*. The macro issues of growth, and the distribution of income between wages and profits, were the major preoccupation of all the great classical economists including Adam Smith, Thomas Malthus, John Stuart Mill, David Ricardo and Karl Marx.

One of Smith's most important contributions was to introduce into economics the notion of increasing returns – a concept that 'new' growth theory (or endogenous growth theory) has recently rediscovered (see chapter 2). In Smith, increasing returns is based on the division of labour. He saw the division of labour, or gains from specialization, as the very basis of a social economy, otherwise everybody might as well be their own Robinson Crusoe doing everything for themselves. And it is the notion of increasing returns, based on the division of labour, that lay at the heart of Smith's optimistic vision of economic progress as a self-generating process, in contrast to the later classical

1

economists, such as Ricardo and Mill, who believed that economies would end up in a stationary state due to diminishing returns in agriculture; and also in contrast to Marx who believed that capitalism would collapse through its own 'inner contradictions' (competition between capitalists reducing the rate of profit; a failure of effective demand as capital is substituted for labour, and the alienation of workers).

The notion of increasing returns may sound a trivial one but it is of profound significance for the way we view economic processes. It is not possible to understand divisions in the world economy, and so-called 'centre–periphery' models of growth and development (between 'north' and 'south' and rich and poor countries), without distinguishing between activities subject to increasing returns on the one hand and diminishing returns on the other. Increasing returns means rising labour productivity and per capita income, and no limits to the employment of labour set by the (subsistence) wage, whereas diminishing returns implies the opposite. Industry is, by and large, an increasing returns activity, while land-based activities, such as agriculture and mining, are diminishing returns activities. Rich, developed countries tend to specialize in increasing returns activities, while poor developing countries tend to specialize in diminishing returns activities. It is almost as simple as that, but not quite!

Adam Smith

If we go back to Adam Smith, he recognized three ways in which the productivity of labour is increased through specialization: first, the increased dexterity or skill of labour through what we now call 'learning by doing'; second, the saving of time which is otherwise lost through switching from one job to another, and third, the greater scope for capital accumulation, that is, the ability to break up complex processes into simpler processes permitting the use of machinery, which raises productivity still further. But the division of labour, or the ability to specialize, depends on the extent of the market. Smith used the example of producing pins. There is no point in installing sophisticated machinery to work on the different processes involved in producing a pin if only a few pins are demanded. Workers may as well produce each pin individually. But if the market is large, there is great scope for economies of scale. The extent of the market, however, depends in turn on the division of labour because this determines the level of productivity, per capita income and purchasing power. We have here an interdependent and circular process. The division of labour depends on the extent of the market, but the extent of the market depends on the division of labour.

Smith recognizes, however, that the process he described was much more a feature of industry than agriculture. He says explicitly:

the nature of agriculture, indeed, does not admit of
so many subdivisions of labour, nor of so complete a
separation of one business from another, as manufactures.
It is impossible to separate so entirely the business of the
grazier from that of the corn farmer, as the trade of the
carpenter is commonly separated from that of the smith.
(p. 16)

There is not the scope for increasing returns in
agriculture. Indeed, if land is a fixed factor of
production, there will be diminishing returns to
labour – one of the few incontrovertible laws of
economics, as Keynes once said.

As far as the extent of the market is concerned,
Smith also recognized the importance of exports,
as we do today particularly for small countries.
Exports provide a 'vent for surplus'; that is, an
outlet for surplus commodities that otherwise
would go unsold. There is a limit to which
indigenous populations can consume fish, bananas
and coconuts, or can use copper, diamonds and
oil:

without an extensive foreign market, [manufacturers]
could not well flourish, either in countries so moderately
extensive as to afford but a narrow home market; or in
countries where the communication between one province
and another [is] so difficult as to render it impossible for
the goods of any particular place to enjoy the whole of
that home market which the country can afford (p. 680)

This vision of Smith of growth and development
as a cumulative interactive process based on
the division of labour and increasing returns in
industry lay effectively dormant until the American

economist, Allyn Young, based at the London School of Economics, revived it in a neglected but profound paper in 1928 entitled 'Increasing Returns and Economic Progress' (another paper rediscovered by 'new' growth theory). As Young observed:

> Adam Smith's famous theorem amounts to saying that the division of labour depends in large part on the division of labour. [But] this is more than mere tautology. It means that the counter forces which are continually defeating the forces which make for equilibrium are more pervasive and more deeply rooted than we commonly realise – change becomes progressive and propagates itself in a cumulative way.

In Young, increasing returns are not simply confined to factors which raise productivity *within* individual industries, but are related to the output of all industries which he argues must be seen as an interrelated whole. For example, a larger market for one good may make it profitable to use more machinery in its production, which reduces the cost of the good *and* the cost of machinery which then makes the use of machinery profitable in other industries, and so on. In other words, a larger market for one good confers a positive externality on others. Under certain conditions, change will become progressive and propagate itself in a cumulative way: the precise conditions being increasing returns and an elastic demand for products so that, as their exchange value falls, proportionately more is bought. Let us consider a simple example of Young's vision of increasing returns as a macro phenomenon. Take the steel and textile industries, both subject to increasing returns and producing price-elastic products. As the supply of steel increases, its relative price falls. If demand is elastic textile producers demand proportionately more steel. Textile production increases and its relative price then falls. If demand is elastic steel producers demand proportionately more textiles, and so on. As Young says: 'under certain circumstances there are no limits to the process of expansion except the limits beyond which demand is not elastic and returns do not increase'.

This process could not happen with diminishing returns activities, such as primary products, with demand price inelastic. No wonder levels of development, both historically and today, seem to be associated with the process of industrialization. There is, indeed, a strong association across countries between the level of per capita income and the share of industry in GDP, and also a strong association across countries between industrial growth and the growth of GDP (see Chapter 3).

Allyn Young's 1928 vision also got lost until economists such as Gunnar Myrdal (Swedish Nobel Prize winner in economics), Albert Hirschman and Nicholas Kaldor (a pupil of Young at the LSE, and later joint-architect of the Cambridge post-Keynesian school of economists) started to develop non-equilibrium models of the development process in such books as *Economic*

Theory and Underdeveloped Regions (Myrdal, 1957); *Strategy of Economic Development* (Hirschman, 1958), and *Economics without Equilibrium* (Kaldor, 1985). Kaldor used to joke that economics went wrong after Chapter 4 of Book I of the *Wealth of Nations* (1776) when Adam Smith abandoned the assumption of increasing returns in favour of constant returns, and the foundations for general equilibrium theory were laid: but foundations totally inappropriate for analysing the dynamics of growth and change.

The Classical Pessimists

The prevailing classical view after Smith was very pessimistic about the process of economic development, which led the historian, Thomas Carlyle, to describe economics as the dismal science – not a view shared by present readers, I hope! The first of the pessimists was Thomas Malthus, who wrote his famous *Essay on the Principle of Population* in 1798, in which he claimed that there is a 'tendency in all animated life to increase beyond the nourishment prepared for it'. According to Malthus, 'population, when unchecked, goes on doubling itself every 25 years, or increases in a geometric ratio [whereas] it may be fairly said – that the means of subsistence increases in an arithmetical ratio'. Taking the world as a whole, therefore, Malthus concludes that 'the human species would increase (if unchecked) as the numbers 1, 2, 4, 8, 16, 32, 64, 128, 256 and subsistence as 1, 2, 3, 4, 5,

6, 7, 8, 9'. This implies, of course, a diminishing proportional rate of increase of food production, or diminishing returns to agriculture. The result of this imbalance between food supply and population will be that living standards oscillate around a subsistence level, with rising living standards leading to more children, which then reduces living standards again.

This Malthusian vision forms the basis in the development literature of models of the low-level equilibrium trap associated originally with Nelson (1956) and Leibenstein (1957), and models of the big push to escape from it. The ghost of Malthus does, indeed, still haunt many Third World countries, although it has to be said that, for the world as a whole, food production has grown much faster than population for at least the last century. The reason is that technical progress, always underestimated by the classical pessimists, has offset diminishing returns, leading to substantial increases in productivity, particularly in Europe and North America, but also in developing countries that experienced a 'green revolution'.

Another of the great classical pessimists was David Ricardo. In 1817 he published his *Principles of Political Economy and Taxation*, in which he predicted that capitalist economies would end up in a stationary state with no capital accumulation and therefore no growth, also due to diminishing returns in agriculture. In Ricardo's model, capital accumulation is determined by profits, but profits get squeezed between subsistence wages and the payment of rent to landowners which increases as the price of food increases owing to diminishing returns to land and rising marginal cost. As the profit rate in agriculture falls, capital shifts to industry, causing the profit rate to decline there too. In industry, profits also get squeezed because the subsistence wage rises in terms of food. As profits fall to zero, capital accumulation ceases, heralding the stationary state. Ricardo recognized that the cheap import of food could delay the stationary state, and as an industrialist and politician, as well as an economist, he campaigned vigorously for the repeal of the Corn Laws in England which protected British farmers. Arthur Lewis's famous model economic development with unlimited supplies of labour (Lewis, 1954) is a classical Ricardian model, but one where the industrial wage stays the same as long as surplus labour exists. Ricardo's pessimism has also been confounded by technical progress, and the stationary state has never appeared on the horizon, except, perhaps, in Africa in recent times, but the causes there are different and complex, related to political failure.

Karl Marx in his famous book, *Das Kapital* (1867), also predicted crisis due to falling profits, but through a different mechanism related to competition between capitalists, overproduction and social upheaval. The wages of labour are determined institutionally, and profit (or surplus value, which only labour can create) is the difference between output per man and the wage rate. The rate of profit is given by $s/(v+c)$ or $(s/v)/(1+c/v)$, where s is surplus value, c is 'constant' capital, v is 'variable' capital (the wage bill), and c/v is defined as the organic composition of capital. The latter is assumed to rise through time, and as it does so, the rate of profit will fall unless the rate of surplus value rises. As long as surplus labour (or what Marx called a 'reserve army of unemployed') exists there is no problem, but Marx predicted that, as capital accumulation takes place, the reserve army will disappear, driving wages up and profits down. The capitalists' response is either to attempt to keep wages down (the immiseration of workers) leading to social conflict, or to substitute more capital for labour, which raises the organic composition of capital and worsens the problem of a falling profit rate. Moreover, as labour is replaced, it cannot consume all the goods produced, and there is a failure of effective demand, or a 'realization crisis', as Marx called it. Capitalism collapses through its own 'inner contradictions', and power passes to the working classes.

Classical models of growth and distribution still form an integral part of growth and development theory, particularly the emphasis on the capitalist surplus for investment, but the gloomy prognostications of the classical economists have not materialized, at least for the capitalist world as a whole. As said before, what is wrong with Malthus and Ricardo is that they both underestimated the strength of technical progress in agriculture as an offset to diminishing returns. What is wrong with

Marx is that he first of all confused money and real wages, and secondly underestimated the effect of technical progress in industry on the productivity of labour. A rise in money wages as labour becomes scarcer does not necessarily mean a rise in real wages; and a rise in real wages could be offset by a rise in productivity, leaving the rate of profit unchanged. In other words, in a growing economy, there is no necessary conflict between wages and the rate of profit.

For nearly 60 years after Marx's death in 1883, growth and development theory lay virtually dormant, until it was revived by the British economist (Sir) Roy Harrod in 1939 in a classic article, 'An Essay in Dynamic Theory'. In the late 19th and early 20th centuries, economics was dominated by neoclassical value theory under the influence of Jevons, Walras and particularly Alfred Marshall's *Principles of Economics*, published in 1890. Growth and development was regarded as an evolutionary natural process akin to biological developments in the natural world. All this changed in 1939 with Harrod's article, which led to the development of what came to be called the Harrod–Domar growth model (named after Evesey Domar as well, who derived independently Harrod's fundamental result in 1947 but in a different way (Domar, 1947)). The model has played a major part in thinking about development issues ever since, and is still widely used as a planning framework in developing countries.

Neoclassical growth theory was born as a reaction to the Harrod–Domar model, and 'new' growth theory developed as a reaction to neoclassical growth theory.

Harrod–Domar Growth Model

Harrod was one of the most original and versatile economists of the 20th century. He was the inventor of the marginal revenue product curve in micro theory; the life cycle hypothesis of saving and the absorption approach to the balance of payments in macro theory; the biographer of Keynes; the author of a book on inductive logic; as well as the originator of modern growth theory.

Harrod's 1939 model was an extension of Keynes's static equilibrium analysis of *The General Theory*. The question Harrod asked was: if the condition for a static equilibrium is that plans to invest must equal plans to save, what must be the *rate of growth of income* for this equilibrium condition to hold in a growing economy through time? Moreover, is there any guarantee that this required rate of growth will prevail?

Harrod introduced three different growth concepts: the actual growth rate (g_a); the warranted growth rate (g_w) and the natural growth rate (g_n). The actual growth rate is defined as $g_a = s/c$, where s is the savings ratio and c is the actual incremental capital–output ratio (that is, the amount of extra capital accumulation or investment associated with a unit increase in output). This expression is definitionally true because in the national income accounts, savings and investment are equal. Thus $s/c = (S/Y)/(I/\Delta Y) = (\Delta Y/Y)$, where S is saving, I is investment, Y is output, and $\Delta Y/Y$ is the growth rate (g_a).

This rate of growth, however, does not necessarily guarantee a moving equilibrium through time in the sense that it induces just enough investment to match *planned* saving. Harrod called this rate the warranted growth rate. Formally, it is the rate that keeps capital fully employed, so that there is no overproduction or underproduction, and manufacturers are therefore willing to carry on investment in the future at the same rate as in the past. How is this rate determined? The demand for investment is given by an accelerator mechanism (or what Harrod called 'the relation') with planned investment (I_p) a function of the change in output, so that $I_p = c_r\Delta Y$, where c_r is the required incremental capital–output ratio at a given rate of interest, determined by technological conditions. Planned saving (S_p) is a function of income so that $S_p = sY$ where s is the propensity to save. Setting planned investment equal to planned saving gives $c_r\Delta Y = sY$ or $\Delta Y/Y = s/c_r$, which equals the warranted growth rate (g_w). For dynamic equilibrium, output must grow at the rate s/c_r. If not, the economic system will be cumulatively unstable. If actual growth exceeds the warranted growth rate, plans to invest will exceed plans to save; and the actual growth rate is pushed even further above the warranted rate. Contrariwise, if actual growth is less than the warranted rate, plans to invest will be less than plans to save and growth will fall further below the warranted rate. This is the Harrod instability problem. Economies appeared to be poised on a 'knife-edge'. Any departure from equilibrium, instead of being self-righting, will be self-aggravating.

The American economist, Evesey Domar, working independently of Harrod, also arrived at Harrod's central conclusion by a different route – hence the linking of their two names. What Domar realized was that investment both increases demand via the Keynesian multiplier and also increases supply by expanding capacity. So the question he posed was: what is the rate of growth of investment that will guarantee that demand matches supply? The crucial rate of growth of investment can be derived in the following way. A change in the level of investment increases demand by $\Delta Y_d = \Delta I / s$, and investment itself increases supply by $\Delta Y_s = I\sigma$, where σ is the productivity of capital ($\Delta Y / I$). Therefore, for $\Delta Y_d = \Delta Y_s$ we must have $\Delta I / s = I\sigma$, or $\Delta I / I = s\sigma$. That is to say, investment must grow at a rate equal to the product of the savings ratio and the productivity of investment. With a constant savings–investment ratio, this implies output growth at the rate $s\sigma$. Since $\sigma = 1/c_r$ (at full employment), the Harrod and Domar result for equilibrium growth is the same.

Even if the actual and warranted growth rates are equal, however, guaranteeing the full utiliza-tion of capital, this does not guarantee the full utilization of labour which depends on the natural rate of growth (g_n) made up of two components: the growth of the labour force (l) and the growth of labour productivity (t), both exogenously given. The sum of the two gives the growth of the labour force in efficiency units. If all labour is to be employed, the actual growth rate must match the natural rate. If the actual growth rate falls below the natural rate there will be growing unemployment of the structural variety.

It should be clear that the full employment of both capital and labour requires that $g_a = g_w = g_n$; a happy coincidental state of affairs that Joan Robinson once coined 'the golden age' to emphazise its mythical nature.

Where do the developing countries fit into this story? The short-run (trade cycle) problem is the relation between g_a and g_w, and we will not say more about this here. The long-run problem is the relation between g_w and g_n, or the relation between the growth of capital and the growth of the labour force in efficiency units. Almost certainly, in most developing countries, g_n exceeds g_w. Labour force growth (determined by population growth) may be 2 per cent per annum, and productivity growth 3 per cent per annum, giving a natural growth rate of 5 per cent. If the *net* savings ratio is 9 per cent and the required incremental capital–output ratio is 3, the warranted growth rate is only 3 per cent. Therefore $g_n > g_w$. This has two main consequences. Firstly, it means that the effective labour force is growing faster than capital accumulation,

so that with fixed coefficients of production there
will be unemployment of the structural variety.
Secondly, it means that plans to invest will exceed
plans to save, because if the economy could grow
at 5 per cent there are profitable investment oppor-
tunities for more than 9 per cent saving, and there
will be inflationary pressure. Hence the simultaneous existence of unemployment and inflation
in developing countries is not a paradox; it is the
outcome of an inequality between the natural and
warranted growth rates.

A good deal of development policy can be
understood and considered within this Harrod
framework. The task is to bring g_n and g_w closer
together; to reduce g_n and to increase g_w. The only
feasible way to reduce the growth of the labour
force is to reduce population growth. The Harrod
model provides a rationale for population control.
A second way to reduce g_n is to reduce the rate
of labour-saving technical progress, but this has
the serious drawback of reducing the growth of
living standards. A rise in g_w could be brought
about by increases in the savings ratio. This is
what monetary and fiscal policy programmes are
designed to do, with emphasis on tax reform and
policies of financial liberalization. A rise in g_w could
also come about if the capital–output ratio was
reduced by countries using more labour-intensive
techniques of production. There is a continuing
debate on the choice of appropriate techniques in
developing countries, and whether more labour-

intensive techniques could be employed without the sacrifice of output or saving.

The Harrod (and Domar) model provided the starting point for the great debates in growth economics that preoccupied large sections of the economics profession for at least three decades between the mid-1950s and the 1980s. The battle-lines were drawn up between the neoclassical growth school on the one hand, based in Cambridge, Massachusetts, USA, with the major protagonists being Robert Solow, Paul Samuelson and Franco Modigliani, and the Keynesian growth school on the other, based in Cambridge, England, with the major protagonists being Nicholas Kaldor, Joan Robinson, Richard Kahn and Luigi Pasinetti. What was immediately apparent to both camps was that, if the Harrod–Domar model was a representation of the real world, all economies, rich and poor, capitalist and communist, would be in for a bumpy ride. The variables and parameters determining g_n and g_w were all independently given, and there were apparently no *automatic* mechanisms for bringing the two rates of growth into line to provide the basis for steady long-run growth at the natural rate. The task that both conflicting camps set themselves was to develop mechanisms to reconcile divergences between g_n and g_w.

The Cambridge, England camp focused on the savings ratio, making it a function of the distribution of income between wages and profits which in turn was assumed to be related to whether the economy was in boom or slump. Specifically, in their model the propensity to save out of profits is assumed to be higher than out of wages, and the share of profits in national income is assumed to rise during booms and fall during slumps. Therefore, if g_n exceeds g_w, generating a boom, the share of profits rises and the savings ratio will rise, raising g_w towards g_n. The only constraint might be an 'inflation barrier' caused by workers not being willing to see the share of wages fall below a certain minimum. Conversely, if g_n is less than g_w, generating a slump, the share of profits falls and the savings ratio falls, lowering g_w towards g_n. The only limit here might be a minimum rate of profit acceptable to entrepreneurs which sets a limit to the fall in the share of profits.

The Cambridge, Massachusetts camp focused on the capital–output ratio, arguing that, if the labour force grows faster than capital, the price mechanism will operate in such a way as to induce the use of more labour intensive techniques, and vice versa. Thus, if g_n exceeds g_w, the capital–output ratio will fall, raising g_w to g_n. If g_n is less than g_w, the capital–output ratio will rise, lowering g_w to g_n. This neoclassical adjustment mechanism, however, presupposes two things: firstly, that the relative price of labour and capital are flexible enough, and secondly that there is a spectrum of techniques to choose from so that economies can move easily and smoothly along a continuous production function relating output to the factor inputs, capital and labour. If this is true, economies can achieve a growth equilibrium at the natural rate (see Chapter 2).

Out of the neoclassical model, however, came the extraordinary counterintuitive conclusion that investment does not matter for long-run growth because the natural rate depends on the growth of the labour force and labour productivity (determined by technical progress) and both are *exogenously* determined. Any increase in a country's saving or investment ratio would be offset by an increase in the capital–output ratio, leaving the long-run growth rate unchanged. The argument depends crucially, however, on the productivity of capital falling as the capital to labour ratio rises. In other words, it depends on the assumption of *diminishing returns to capital*. This is the neoclassical story that 'new' endogenous growth theory objects to. If there are mechanisms which keep the productivity of capital from falling as more investment takes place, then the investment ratio will matter for long-run growth, and growth is endogenous in this sense; that is, growth is not simply determined by the exogenous growth of the labour force in efficiency units.

In the next chapter we consider in more detail the assumptions and predictions of the neoclassical model, and the criticisms made of it. We then look at the challenge of 'new' growth theory, and we are critical of this too.

2. Neoclassical and 'new' growth theory: a critique

Our task in this chapter is to outline formally the assumptions and predictions of neoclassical growth theory as a background to showing, firstly, how the neoclassical production function is used for analysing growth rate differences between countries, and its weaknesses; and secondly, how neoclassical growth theory forms the basis for 'new' endogenous growth theory – the only major difference being that the assumption of diminishing returns to capital is relaxed, so that 'new' growth theory is subject to the same major criticisms as conventional neoclassical theory as far as analysing and understanding growth rate differences between countries is concerned.

The Neoclassical Model

The neoclassical growth model is based on three key assumptions. The first is that the labour force (l) and labour-saving technical progress (t) grow at a constant *exogenous* rate. The second assumption is that all saving is invested: $S = I = sY$. There is no independent investment function. The third assumption is that output is a function of capital and labour, where the production function exhibits constant returns to scale, and diminishing returns to individual factors of production. The most commonly used neoclassical production function, with constant returns to scale, is the so-called Cobb–Douglas production function, named after Charles Cobb, a mathematician, and Paul Douglas, a well-known Chicago economist before World War II (who later became a US senator). The function takes the form:

$$Y = TK^{\alpha}L^{1-\alpha}, \tag{2.1}$$

where Y is output, K is capital, L is labour, T is the level of technology, α is the elasticity of output with respect to capital and $1-\alpha$ is the elasticity of output with respect to labour. Obviously $\alpha + (1-\alpha) = 1$ (the assumption of constant returns to scale), so that a 1 per cent increase in capital and labour leads to a 1 per cent increase in output.

To consider the predictions of the model, it is convenient to transform equation (2.1) into its 'labour-intensive' form by dividing both sides by L, so that the dependent variable is output per head, and the independent variables are the level of technology and capital per head.

$$Y/L = (TK^{\alpha}L^{1-\alpha})/L = T(K/L)^{\alpha}$$

or

$$q = T(k)^{\alpha} \tag{2.2}$$

where q is output per head and k is capital per head.

The basic predictions of the neoclassical model, which can be shown diagrammatically (see below), are as follows:

1. in the steady state, the *level* of output per head (q) is positively related to the savings– investment ratio and negatively related to the growth of population (or labour force);
2. the *growth of output* is *independent* of the savings– investment ratio and is determined by the exogenously given rate of growth of the labour force in efficiency units ($l + t$). This is because a higher savings–investment ratio is offset by a higher capital–output ratio (or a lower productivity of capital) owing to the assumption of diminishing returns to capital;
3. given identical tastes and preferences (that is, the same savings ratio) and technology (that is, production function), there will be an *inverse* relation across countries between the capital–labour ratio and the productivity of capital, so that poor countries should grow faster than rich countries, leading to the *convergence* of per capita incomes across the world.

Figure 2.1 illustrates the first two predictions.

The production function, $q = f(k)$, with diminishing returns to capital, comes from equation (2.2). The ray from the origin with slope $(l + t)/s$ gives points of equality between the rate of growth of

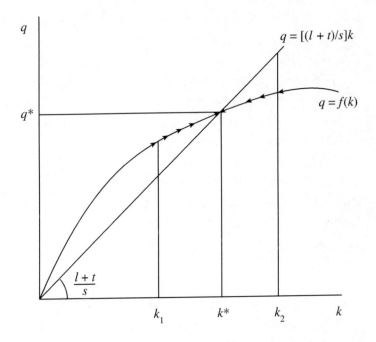

Figure 2.1

capital and labour measured in efficiency units.[1] Only at k^* is the level of output per head such as to give a rate of growth of capital equal to the rate of growth of the labour force. To the left of $k^*(k_1)$, the growth of capital is greater than the growth of labour, and economies are assumed to move along their smooth production function towards k^* using more capital-intensive methods of production. To the right of $k^*(k_2)$, the growth of capital is less than the growth of labour, and economies are assumed to use more labour-intensive techniques of production. At k^*, where the capital to labour ratio is in equilibrium, output per head will also be in equilibrium at q^*. It can be seen from the figure that a rise in the savings ratio (s) pivots downwards the ray from the origin and raises the equilibrium k and raises the *level* of q, but does not affect the growth rate of the economy. It can also be seen that the level of q will be inversely related to the rate of growth of the labour force because a rise in l pivots upwards the ray from the origin.

The explanation for convergence of per capita income across countries can be seen from the formula for the capital–output ratio:

$$K/Y = (K/L)\,(L/Y). \qquad (2.3)$$

If there is diminishing returns to capital, a higher K/L will not be offset by a higher Y/L ratio, and therefore K/Y will be higher. Thus, if the savings–investment ratio is the same across countries, rich countries with a higher K/L ratio should grow more slowly than poor countries with a lower K/L because the productivity of capital is lower in the former case than in the latter.

What major criticisms can be made of this model, apart from the empirical fact that across the world we do not observe the convergence of living standards? The fundamental point to be made at this stage is that the neoclassical model is a *supply-oriented* model *par excellence*. First, demand never enters the picture. Saving leads to investment, so that supply creates its own demand. The neoclassical model of growth takes us back to a pre-Keynesian world where demand does not matter for an understanding of the determination of the level of output (and, by implication, the growth of output). Secondly, factors of production and technical progress are treated as *exogenously* determined, unresponsive to demand. But, by and large, the demand for factors of production is a derived demand, derived from the growth of output itself. Much technical progress and labour productivity growth is also induced by the growth of output itself (see later).

The assumption of exogeneity of factor supplies is no more apparent than in the studies that use the aggregate production function for analysing growth rate differences between countries; an approach pioneered by Abramovitz (1956) and Solow (1957) and still widely utilized. Let us consider this approach and comment on its limitations.

Using the Production Function for Analysing Growth Differences

If we go back to the Cobb–Douglas production function in equation (2.1), it is easy to see how it can be used for analysing the sources of growth; that is, decomposing a country's growth rate into the contribution of capital, labour and technical progress. The question is, how useful is it for a proper *understanding* of the growth performance of countries if the main inputs into the growth process are not exogenous but *endogenous*?

The function in equation (2.1) is made operational by taking logarithms of the variables and differentiating with respect to time, which gives:

$$y = t + \alpha(k) + (1 - \alpha)l, \qquad (2.4)$$

or in labour-intensive form:

$$y - l = t + \alpha (k - l), \qquad (2.5)$$

where lower-case letters represent rates of growth of the variables.

Given estimates of α and $(1 - \alpha)$, the contribution of capital growth and labour force growth to any measured growth rate can be estimated, leaving the contribution of technical progress as a residual. For example, suppose $y = 5\%$, $k = 5\%$, $l = 2\%$, $\alpha = 0.3$ and $(1 - \alpha) = 0.7$. The contribution of capital to growth is then $(0.3) (5\%) = 1.5$ percentage points or 30 per cent; the contribution of labour is $(0.7) (2\%) = 1.4$ percentage points or 28 per cent, leaving the contribution of technical progress as $5\% - 2.9\% = 2.1\%$ or 42 per cent.

Solow (1957) was the first to use the labour-intensive form of the Cobb–Douglas production function in analysing the growth performance of the US economy over the previous 50 years, and concluded that only 10 per cent of the growth of output per man could be 'explained' by the growth of capital per man, leaving 90 per cent of growth to be 'explained' by various forms of technical progress. Denison (1962, 1967) used the same production function approach, or growth accounting framework, to study growth performance in the USA and between the countries of Europe, disaggregating the technical progress term (or residual) into various component parts. Maddison (1970) used the approach to study growth rate differences between developing countries. Since this early research, there has been a mass of other studies too extensive to survey here (however, see Felipe, 1999), but two recent studies may be mentioned as illustrative. The World Bank (1991) did a study of 68 countries showing capital accumulation to be of prime importance, with technical progress minimal. This seems to be the central conclusion for developing countries in contrast to developed countries. Secondly, there is the controversial study by Alwyn Young (1995) of the four East Asian 'dragons' of Hong Kong, Singapore, South Korea and Taiwan which also shows that most of the growth in these countries can be explained by the growth of factor inputs and not technical progress, so that, according to Young, there has been no growth miracle in these countries – contrary to the conventional wisdom.

Before accepting this conclusion, however, the observer still has to explain why there was such a rapid growth of factor inputs, and it is this point which exposes the fundamental weakness of the production function approach to the analysis of growth performance. Inputs are not manna from heaven dropped by God. Something 'miraculous' must have been driving these economies, to

which input growth responded. On closer
inspection, what distinguishes these countries is
their outward orientation and relentless search
for export markets, and their remarkable growth
of exports which confers benefits on an economy
from both the demand and the supply side (see
Chapter 4). This exposes another weakness of
neoclassical growth theory and that is that the
models are closed. There is no trade in these
simple models, and no balance of payments to
worry about. They are supply-oriented, supply-
driven, closed economy models unsuitable for
the analysis of open economies in which foreign
exchange is invariably a scarce resource acting to
constrain the growth process. We return to this
topic in Chapters 4 and 5, but first we must look
at the challenge of 'new' growth theory.

'New' Endogenous Growth Theory

Since the mid-1980s there has been an outpouring
of literature and research on the applied economics
of growth, attempting to understand and explain
differences in output growth and living standards
across countries of the world – most inspired by
so-called 'new' growth theory or endogenous
growth theory. This spate of studies seems to have
been prompted by a number of factors: firstly, by
the increased concern with the economic performance of poorer parts of the world, and particularly
major differences between continents and between
countries, with South East Asia forging ahead,

Africa left behind and South America somewhere in the middle; secondly, by the increased availability of standardized data on which to do research (Summers and Heston, 1991); and thirdly, by studies showing *no convergence* of per capita incomes in the world economy (for example, Baumol, 1986), contrary to the prediction of neoclassical growth theory based on the assumption of diminishing returns to capital.

If there are not diminishing returns to capital – but, say, constant returns – a higher capital–labour ratio will be exactly offset by a higher output per head,[2] and the capital–output ratio will not be higher in capital-rich countries than in capital-poor countries, and the savings–investment ratio will therefore matter for long-run growth. Growth is endogenously determined in this sense and not simply determined by the exogenous rate of growth of the labour force and technical progress. This is the starting point for 'new', endogenous growth theory which seeks an explanation of *why* there has not been a convergence of living standards in the world economy.

The explanation of 'new' growth theory is that there are forces at work which prevent the marginal product of capital from falling (and the capital–output ratio from rising) as more investment takes place as countries get richer. Paul Romer (1986) first suggested externalities to research and development (R&D) expenditure. Robert Lucas (1988) focuses on externalities to human capital formation (education). Grossman and Helpman (1991) concentrate on technological spillovers from trade and foreign direct investment (FDI). Other economists have stressed the role of infrastructure investment and its complementarity with other types of investment. In fact, it can be seen from the formula for the capital–output ratio that increasing returns to labour for all sorts of reasons could keep the capital–output ratio from rising.

So now let us turn to 'new' growth theory, see what it has to say, see whether it is saying anything new, and consider some of the problems of interpreting the empirical results from testing new growth theory.

The first crude test of new growth theory is to observe whether or not there is an inverse relation across countries between the growth of output per head and the *initial* level of per capita income of countries. If there is, this would be supportive of the neoclassical prediction of convergence. If not, it would be supportive of 'new' growth theory that the marginal product of capital does not decline. This is referred to as the test for beta (β) convergence. It can be said straight away that no global studies find evidence of *unconditional* beta convergence. Virtually all studies find evidence of divergence. The coefficient linking the growth of output per head to the initial level of per capita income is positive, not negative.

Before jumping to the conclusion that this is unequivocal support for 'new' growth theory, however, it must be remembered that the neoclassical prediction of convergence assumes all other things the same across countries: population growth; tastes and preferences (for example, the savings ratio); technology and so on. Since these assumptions are manifestly false, there can never be the presumption of *unconditional* convergence – only *conditional* convergence controlling for differences in all other factors that affect the growth of living standards, including differences in the ratio of investment to GDP and variables that affect the productivity of capital and labour such as education and training, R&D expenditure, trade, macroeconomic performance and political stability. The question is, what happens to the sign on the initial per capita income variable when these control variables are introduced into the equation? If the sign on initial per capita income turns negative, this is supposed to represent a rehabilitation of the neoclassical model. In other words, living standards would converge *if only* levels of investment, education, R&D expenditure and so on were the same in poor countries as rich countries, but they are not! The argument is reminiscent of the way neoclassical economists continue to work with fictitious models of competitive equilibrium in the presence of increasing returns, by treating the latter as externalities (the device originally adopted by Alfred Marshall in 1890). Indeed, most 'new' growth theorists, and particularly Robert Barro (1991), are clearly neoclassical economists in disguise. We will look at the work of Barro and others later, but first let us consider the 'newness' of 'new' growth theory and the interpretation of results.

First, I find it amusing that it seems to have come as a surprise to many members of the economics profession that living standards in the world have not been converging according to the prediction of neoclassical growth theory. Long before the advent of 'new' growth theory, many 'non-orthodox' economists had been pointing to widening divisions in the world economy, and developed models to explain divergence. That is what the centre–periphery models of Prebisch (1950), Myrdal (1957), Hirschman (1958), Seers (1962) and the neo-Marxist school (for example, Emmanuel, 1972; Frank, 1967) were all about, many based on a combination of international trade and increasing returns.

Secondly, it has to be said that many of the ideas of 'new' growth theory are not new at all. Who, apart from strict adherents to the neoclassical model, ever believed that investment did not matter for long-run growth? Kaldor (1957), with his technical progress function, precisely anticipated new growth theory by arguing that technical progress requires capital accumulation and capital accumulation requires technical progress (it is impossible to have one without the other), and his model of growth gives an explanation of why the capital–output ratio stays constant through time despite a rising ratio of capital to labour (see later). On the origins of increasing returns, we could mention Adam Smith and the division of labour (see Chapter 1), Allyn Young and the idea of increasing returns as a macroeconomic phenomenon related to the interaction between activities (see Chapter 1), Kenneth Arrow's model of learning by doing (Arrow, 1962), the work of Schultz (1961) and Denison (1962) on the social returns to education, and the work of Griliches (1958) on the social returns to R&D. We have an endearing tendency in economics to reinvent the wheel.

Thirdly, when it comes to interpreting the empirical results from testing models of new growth theory and convergence, some care needs to be taken. In particular, great care needs to be exercised in interpreting the negative sign on the initial level of per capita income as necessarily rehabilitating the neoclassical model of growth, as for example, Barro (1991) does, because there are other conceptually distinct reasons for expecting a negative sign. Firstly, outside the neoclassical paradigm, there is a whole body of literature that argues that economic growth *should be* inversely related to the initial level of per capita income because, the more backward a country, the greater the scope for *catch-up*; that is, for absorbing a backlog of technology, which represents a shift in the whole production function. Is conditional convergence picking up diminishing returns to capital in the neoclassical sense, or catch-up? The two concepts are conceptually distinct, but not easy to disentangle empirically. Secondly, the negative term could simply be picking up structural change, with poor countries growing faster than rich countries (controlling for other variables) because of a more rapid shift of resources from low productivity to high productivity sectors (for example, from agriculture to industry). How do we discriminate between these hypotheses?

A fourth point concerns the specification of 'new' growth theory in its simplest form as the so-called *AK* model:

$$Y = AK, \qquad (2.6)$$

where A is a constant, which implies a constant proportional relation between output (Y) and capital (K), or constant returns to capital. On close inspection, this specification is none other than the Harrod growth equation $g = s/c$ (see Chapter 1). This can be seen by taking changes in Y and K and dividing by Y, which gives:

$$\Delta Y/Y = A\,\Delta K/Y = A\,(I/Y), \qquad (2.7)$$

where $\Delta Y/Y$ is the growth rate (g); I/Y is the savings–investment ratio (s), and A is the productivity of investment, $\Delta Y/I = 1/c$ or the reciprocal of the incremental capital–output ratio. What this means is that, if the productivity of investment (A) was the same across all countries, there would be a perfect correlation between growth and the investment ratio. If there is not a perfect correlation, then *definitionally* there must be differences across countries in the productivity of capital. All that empirical studies of 'new' growth theory are really doing is trying to explain differences in the productivity of capital across countries (provided the investment ratio is in the equation) in terms of differences in education, R&D expenditure, trade and so on, and initial endowments (see Hussein and Thirlwall, 2000, for further elaboration of this point).

As far as the constancy of the capital–output ratio is concerned, it was pointed out by Kaldor (1957) many years ago, as one of his six stylized facts of economic growth, that, despite capital accumulation and increases in capital per head through time, the capital–output ratio has remained broadly unchanged, implying some form of externalities or increasing returns. It is worth quoting Kaldor in full:

> As regards the process of economic change and development in capitalist societies, I suggest the following 'stylised facts' as a starting point for the construction of theoretical models – (4) steady capital–output ratios over long periods; at least there are no clear long-term trends, either rising or falling, if differences in the degree of capital utilization are allowed for. This implies, or reflects, the near identity in the percentage growth of production and of the capital stock i.e. for the economy as a whole, and over long periods, income and capital tend to grow at the same rate.

Kaldor's explanation lay in his innovation of the technical progress function (TPF) relating the growth of output per man ($\dot{q}$) to the growth of capital per man ($\dot{k}$), as in Figure 2.2.

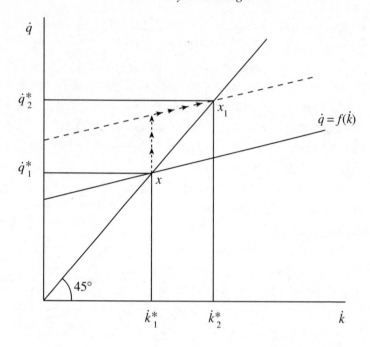

Figure 2.2

The position of the (linear) TPF drawn in Figure 2.2 depends on the exogenous rate of technical progress, and the slope of the function depends on the extent to which technical progress is embodied in capital. Along the 45° line, the capital–output ratio is constant, and the equilibrium growth of output per head is $\dot{q}_1^*$. An upward shift of the function associated with new discoveries, technological breakthroughs and so on will cause the growth of output to exceed the growth of capital, raising the rate of profit and inducing more investment, to give a new equilibrium growth of output per head at $\dot{q}_2^*$ (follow the arrows). An increase in capital accumulation not accompanied by technical progress will simply cause the capital–output ratio to rise. If the capital–output ratio is observed to be constant there must be technological forces at work shifting the function upwards. 'New' growth theory is precisely anticipated.

What applies to countries through time applies *pari passu* to different countries at a point in time, with differences in country growth rates at the same capital–output ratio associated with different technical progress functions. To quote Kaldor again:

> A lower capital–labour ratio does not necessarily imply a lower capital–output ratio – indeed, the reverse is often the case. The countries with the most highly mechanised industries, such as the United States, do not require a higher ratio of capital to output. The capital–output ratio in the United States has been falling over the past 50 years whilst the capital–labour ratio has been steadily rising; and it is lower in the United States today than in the man-ufacturing industries of many underdeveloped countries. (Kaldor, 1972)

In other words, rich and poor countries are simply not on the same production function.

A final point concerns the way that new growth theory models trade. First of all, some of the models and empirical studies do not consider the role of trade at all, as if economies are completely closed. It is hard to imagine how it is possible to explain growth rate differences between countries without reference to trade, and particularly without reference to the balance of payments of countries which constitutes for many developing countries the major constraint on the growth of demand and output (which will reduce the productivity of capital). When a trade variable is included in the model, it is invariably insignificant, or loses its significance when combined with other variables. On the surface, this is a puzzle. It would conflict with the rich historical literature that exists on the relation between trade and growth (Thirlwall, 2000). It would conflict with the voluminous work of the World Bank and other organizations showing the beneficial effects of trade liberalization, and it would undermine the whole thrust of international policy making since World War II, which has been to free up markets and to promote trade in the interests of economic development.

There may be several explanations for the weak results, but I believe the major one is that the trade variable normally taken is the *share* of exports in GDP as a measure of 'openness' which may pick up the static gains from trade and technological spillovers, but not the *dynamic* effects of trade which can only be properly captured by the *growth* of exports which affects demand, both directly and indirectly (by relaxing a balance of payments constraint on demand), and also the supply side of the economy by permitting a faster growth of imports. This point relates to my general criticism of 'new' growth theory that it neglects demand-side variables. When an export growth variable is included in a 'new' growth theory equation, it is highly significant (see Thirlwall and Sanna,1996).

When it comes to evaluating the empirical evidence, only four variables in 'new' growth theory equations appear to be robust (see Levine and Renelt, 1992): the initial level of per capita income, the savings–investment ratio, investment in human capital, and population growth (usually). All other variables are fragile in the sense that, when they are combined with other variables, they lose their significance. The robust variables are ones that growth analysts have stressed for many years, long before the advent of 'new' growth theory. *Plus ça change, plus c'est la même chose.*

Notes

1. This can be seen by rearranging the equation $q = [(l + t)/s]$ k to $qs/k = l + t$, where $q = Y/L$; $s = S/Y = \Delta K/Y$ (since all saving leads to capital accumulation) and $k = K/L$. Therefore $(Y/L)(\Delta K/Y)(L/K) = \Delta K/K = l + t$.
2. Remember $K/Y = (K/L)/(Y/L)$.

3. Manufacturing industry as the engine of growth

The neoclassical approach to economic growth, and its offspring 'new' growth theory, are not only very supply-oriented, treating factor supplies as exogenously given, but are also very aggregative. They treat all sectors of the economy as if they are alike. They do not explicitly pick out any one sector as more important than another. In practice, however, aggregate growth will naturally be related to the rate of expansion of the sector with the most favourable growth characteristics.

There is a lot of historical, empirical evidence to suggest that there is something special about industrial activity, and particularly manufacturing. There seems to be a close association across countries between the level of per capita income and the degree of industrialization, and there also seems to be a close association across countries between the growth of GDP and the growth of manufacturing industry. Countries which are growing fast tend to be those where the share of industry in GDP is rising most rapidly: the so-called 'newly industrializing countries' (the NICs). Is this an accident?

One of the first economists to have seriously addressed this issue is the late Nicholas Kaldor, who argued in many of his writings (see Targetti and Thirlwall, 1989) that it is impossible to understand the growth and development process without taking a sectoral approach, distinguishing between increasing returns activities on the one hand (which he associated with industry) and diminishing returns activities on the other (which he associated with the land-based activities of agriculture and mining). Kaldor first articulated his theory about why growth rates differ in two lectures: one in Cambridge in 1966 entitled *Causes of the Slow Rate of Economic Growth of the United Kingdom* (Kaldor, 1966); the other at Cornell University in the same year entitled *Strategic Factors in Economic Development* (Kaldor, 1967). In these lectures he presented a series of 'laws' or empirical generalizations which attempted to account for growth rate differences between advanced capitalist countries, but which also have applicability to developing countries as well.

There are three laws to focus on, plus a number of subsidiary propositions. The first law is that there exists a strong causal relation between the growth of manufacturing output and the growth of GDP. The second law states that there exists a strong positive causal relation between the growth of manufacturing output and the growth of productivity in manufacturing as a result of static and dynamic returns to scale. This is also known as Verdoorn's Law (see Chapter 1 and later). The third law states that there exists a strong positive causal relation between the rate at which the manufacturing sector expands and the growth of productivity outside the manufacturing sector because of diminishing returns in agriculture and many petty service activities which supply labour to the industrial sector. If the marginal product of labour is below the average product in these sectors, the average product (productivity) will rise as employment is depleted. For this reason, overall GDP growth will tend to slow up as the scope for absorbing labour from diminishing returns activities dries up.

Given these 'laws', the question remains of what determines the growth of the manufacturing sector in the first place. Kaldor's answer is demand coming from agriculture in the early stages of development and export growth in the later stages. These are the two fundamental sources of autonomous demand to match the leakages of income from the industrial sector of food imports from agriculture on the one hand and imports from abroad on the other. A fast growth of exports and output may then set up a virtuous circle of growth with rapid export growth leading to rapid output growth, and rapid output growth leading to fast export growth through the favourable impact of output growth on competitiveness. Other countries find it difficult to break into such virtuous circles, and this is why the polarization between countries occurs. The present north–south divide in the world economy has its origins in the fact that the 'north' contains the first set of countries to industrialize, and only a handful of countries since have managed to challenge their industrial supremacy and to match their living standards.

Kaldor's growth laws can be tested across countries, across regions within countries, across regions and countries using panel data (for example across the regions of the European Union) and for individual countries using time series data (although care has to be taken with the second law not to confuse Verdoorn's Law with Okun's Law, which relates to pro-cyclical variations in productivity over the trade cycle). (See McCombie and Thirlwall, 1994.)

The first test of the first law is to run a regression of the rate of growth of GDP against the rate of growth of manufacturing output and to test for statistical significance. When this is done across countries or regions, the relation is invariably highly significant, but this could be a spurious relation due to the fact that manufacturing output constitutes a sizeable fraction of total output. Side tests therefore need to be undertaken. One is to regress the growth of GDP on the *excess* of the growth of manufacturing output over the growth of non-manufacturing output; another is to regress the growth of non-manufacturing output on the growth of manufacturing output. When these side tests are performed, the first law is generally confirmed. A recent interesting study across the regions of China strongly supports Kaldor's first law (Hansen and Zhang, 1996). For manufacturing to be regarded as special, however, it needs to be shown that GDP growth is not closely related to the growth of other sectors such as agriculture, mining or services. It is hard to find any significant cross-section relation between the growth of GDP and the growth of the agricultural sector. The relation between the growth of GDP and the growth of services is stronger but there is reason to believe that the direction of causation may be the other way round from GDP growth to service growth since the demand for many services is derived from the demand for manufacturing output itself. The question is to what extent service activities have an 'autonomous' existence, and whether they have the production characteristics (for example, static and dynamic scale economies) to induce fast growth. This is still an open question, ripe for further research.

If the first law is accepted, what accounts for the fact that, the faster manufacturing output grows relatively to GDP, the faster GDP seems to grow? Since differences in growth rates are largely accounted for by differences in labour productivity growth (rather than the growth of the labour force), there must be some relationship between the growth of the manufacturing sector and productivity growth in the economy as a whole. This is to be expected for two main reasons. The first is that, wherever industrial production and employment expand, labour resources are drawn from sectors which have open or disguised unemployment (that is, where there is no relation between employment and output), so that labour transference to manufacturing will not cause a diminution in the output of these sectors, and productivity growth increases outside manufacturing (the third law – see below).

The second reason is the existence of increasing returns within industry, both static and dynamic. Static returns relate to the size and scale of production units and are a characteristic largely of manufacturing where, for example, in the process of doubling the linear dimensions of equipment, the surface increases by the square and the volume by the cube (the so-called 'cube rule'). Dynamic economies refer to increasing returns brought about by 'induced' technical progress, learning by doing, external economies in production and so on. Kaldor draws inspiration here from Allyn Young's pioneering paper of 1928, 'Increasing Returns and Economic Progress' with its emphasis on increasing returns as a macroeconomic phenomenon resulting from the interaction between activities in the process of general industrial expansion; ideas now taken up by 'new' growth theory (see Chapter 2). For those interested in the history of economic thought and the intergenerational transmission of ideas (which sometimes take a long time to resurface!), Kaldor was a pupil of Allyn Young at the London School of Economics in 1928 and took a full set of lecture notes from him, including his thoughts on increasing returns (see Thirlwall, 1987a; Sandilands, 1990).

The empirical relation between productivity growth and output growth in manufacturing is known as Verdoorn's Law, following Verdoorn's (1949) paper published in Italian, entitled 'Fattori che Regolano lo Sviluppo della Produttivita del Lavoro'. Interestingly, at the time of publication, Verdoorn was working for Kaldor in the Research and Planning Division of the Economic Commission for Europe in Geneva, of which Kaldor was Director. It was Kaldor who revived Verdoorn's Law in 1966, and it is also known as Kaldor's second law; that is, there is a strong positive causal relation between the growth of manufacturing output and the growth of productivity in manufacturing. In recent years, the relation has been extensively tested across countries (Kaldor, 1966; Michl, 1985); across regions within countries for both developed and developing countries (McCombie and de Ridder, 1983; Fingleton and McCombie, 1998; Leon-Ledesma, 2000a; Hansen and Zhang, 1996) and across industries (McCombie, 1985a). Typically, the estimated Verdoorn coefficient is 0.5, which means that manufacturing output growth is split evenly between induced productivity growth on the one hand and employment growth on the other. The relation is always robust for manufacturing and industry more broadly. The primary sector of agriculture and mining reveals no such relationship, but some studies (for example, Leon-Ledesma, 2000) find evidence of a Verdoorn relation also operating in service activities, although not so strongly.

There are a number of ways in which the Verdoorn relation can be generated. Verdoorn himself derived it from a static Cobb–Douglas production function where the coefficient linking output growth and productivity growth depends on the parameters of the production function, the exogenous rate of technical progress and the rate at which capital is growing relative to the labour force. The Verdoorn coefficient can also be thought of, however, as a much more dynamic relation linked to Kaldor's technical progress function (see Chapter 2) where the coefficient depends on the rate at which capital accumulation is induced by output growth (the accelerator effect), the extent to which technical progress is embodied in capital (reflected in the slope of the technical progress function) and the rate of disembodied technical progress induced by growth (learning by doing).

The estimation of the Verdoorn relation, by regressing productivity growth on output growth, is not without its critics, however, because the question has been raised, quite rightly, of what is cause and what is effect. Some argue that the direction of causation could be from fast productivity growth to fast output growth because fast productivity growth causes demand to expand faster through improved competitiveness. In this (opposite) view, all productivity growth would be autonomous; none induced by output growth itself. Also, for the mechanism to work, the price elasticities of demand would have to be relatively high and wage growth would have to lag behind productivity growth for relative prices to fall. Kaldor did not deny the reverse causation argument – indeed it is part of his export-led growth model (see Chapter 4) – but his argument was always that it would be very difficult to explain such large differences in productivity growth in the same industry over the same time period in different countries without reference to the growth of output itself. To assume that all productivity growth is autonomous would be a denial of the existence of dynamic scale economies and increasing returns. The two-way relation between output growth and productivity growth does mean, however, that the Verdoorn relation should be estimated using simultaneous equation methods to avoid biased estimates of the Verdoorn coefficient.

Whether or not Verdoorn's Law holds, it is not, contrary to the popular view, an indispensable element of the complete Kaldor model. Even in the absence of induced productivity growth in the manufacturing sector (which is difficult to believe) the growth of industry would still be the governing factor determining overall output growth as long as resources used by industry represent a net addition to output either because they would otherwise have been unused or because of diminishing returns elsewhere, or because industry generates its own resources in a way that other sectors do not by the reinvestment of profits. This leads on to Kaldor's third law which states that, the faster the growth of manufacturing output, the faster the rate of labour transference from non-manufacturing, so that productivity growth in non-manufacturing is negatively associated with the growth of employment outside manufacturing. In practice, it is difficult to measure productivity growth in many non-manufacturing activities because output can only be measured by inputs. But it is possible to relate the *overall* rate of productivity growth in the economy as a whole to employment growth in non-manufacturing, controlling for differences in the growth of manufacturing employment or output. When this is done, Kaldor's third law is generally supported. The study referred to earlier across the regions of China by Hansen and Zhang estimates the following equation:

$$p = 0.02 + 0.49 \, (g_m) - 0.82 \, (e_{nm}) \qquad (3.1)$$
$$(16.4) \qquad (5.4)$$

where p is overall productivity growth; g_m is the growth of manufacturing output and e_{nm} is the growth of employment in non-manufacturing. The sign on e_{nm} is negative and significant, as hypothesized, and the sign on g_m is positive and significant (bracketed terms are t values).

There are a number of subsidiary propositions which complete Kaldor's wide vision of the growth and development process. Following on from the third law, as surplus labour becomes exhausted in the non-manufacturing sector, and productivity levels tend to equalize across sectors, the degree of overall productivity growth induced by manufacturing output growth is likely to diminish. This is why country growth rates tend to be fastest in the take-off stage of development and decelerate in maturity (to use Rostow's terminology). It is in this sense that countries at a high level of development may suffer from a 'labour shortage', not in the sense that manufacturing output growth itself is constrained by a shortage of labour because labour is a very elastic factor of production, as we shall argue in Chapter 6. The manufacturing sector can always get the labour it wants, although it may have to pay a higher real wage which eats into profits and investment (*à la* Lewis and Marx). What may constrain manufacturing output growth is not a shortage of labour but demand from agriculture in the early stages of development and exports in the later stages. A nascent industrial sector needs a market to sell to. In the pre-take-off stage of development, agriculture is by far the largest 'external' sector; hence the importance of rising agricultural productivity to provide the purchasing power and growing market for industrial goods.

Kaldor's two-sector model of agriculture and industry (Kaldor, 1996; Thirlwall, 1986) shows the importance of establishing an equilibrium terms of trade between the two sectors if the growth of the economy is to be maximized, so that industrial growth is neither supply-constrained because agricultural prices are too high relative to industrial prices, or demand constrained because they are too low. Through time, however, the importance of agriculture as an autonomous market for industrial goods will diminish and exports will take over, and a fast growth of exports and industrial output will tend to set up a virtuous circle of growth working through Verdoorn's Law and other feedback, reinforcing mechanisms. Fast export growth leads to fast output growth; fast export growth depends on competitiveness and the growth of world income; competitiveness depends on the relationship between wage growth and productivity growth; and fast productivity growth depends on fast output growth. The circle is complete.

I shall outline this model more fully in the next chapter. Suffice it to say, at this point, that a country ignores the performance of its manufacturing sector at its peril, but the foundations must first be laid for the manufacturing sector to prosper. Balanced growth is required between industry and agriculture, and between internal growth and the traded goods sector if balance of payments problems are to be avoided. It is to the role of exports and the balance of payments that we now turn.

4. A demand-oriented approach to economic growth: export-led growth models

In Chapter 2 it was argued that 'new' growth theory is an improvement on old (neoclassical) growth theory in the sense that it can explain why we do not observe convergence in the world economy, but 'new' growth theory is still open to the same criticism as old growth theory; that it is *supply-oriented*. Moreover, 'new' growth theory is not the only model in town to explain divergent trends in the world economy. In neoclassical theory, output growth is a function of factor inputs and factor productivity with no recognition that factor inputs are endogenous, and that factor productivity growth may also be a function of the pressure of demand in an economy. In practice, labour is a derived demand, derived from the demand for output itself. Capital is a produced means of production, and is therefore as much a consequence of the growth of output as its cause. Factor productivity growth will be endogenous if there are static and dynamic returns to scale.

As a starting point for the analysis of growth, therefore, it would seem just as sensible, if not more so, to take a (Keynesian) demand-oriented approach to growth and ask what are the major constraints on demand, and assume that demand constraints generally bite long before supply constraints become operative. In static macro theory, students are taught that national income (or output) is the sum of consumption expenditure, investment and exports, minus imports. In growth analysis, why not teach that national income growth is the weighted sum of the growth of consumption, investment and the balance between exports and imports, and proceed from there? If we take this approach, the role of exports is immediately apparent. Exports differ from other components of demand in three important respects. Firstly, exports are the only true component of autonomous demand in an economic system, in the sense of demand emanating from outside the system. This is very important to bear in mind. The major part of consumption and investment demand is dependent on the growth of income itself. Secondly, exports are the only component of demand that can pay for the import requirements for growth. It may be possible to initiate consumption-led growth, investment-led growth or government expenditure-led growth for a short time, but each of these components of demand has an import content (that is why imports are subtracted in the national income equation). If there are no export earnings to pay for the import content of other components of expenditure, demand will

have to be constrained. In this respect, exports
are of great significance if balance of payments
equilibrium on current account is a long-run
requirement. What it means is that exports have
not only a direct effect on demand, but also an
indirect effect by allowing all other components
of demand to rise faster than otherwise would be
the case. This is the idea of the Hicks supermulti-
plier (Hicks, 1950; McCombie, 1985b) in which the
rate of growth of an economy becomes attuned
to the rate of growth of the dominant component
of autonomous demand, which in the case of the
open economy is exports. The third important
aspect of exports is that imports (permitted by
exports) may be more productive than domestic
resources because certain crucial goods necessary
for development (such as capital goods) are not
produced domestically. This is the supply-side
argument for export-led growth.

It can then be shown that, if there are increasing
returns and induced productivity growth, export
growth can set up a virtuous circle of growth which
leads into centre–periphery models of growth and
development which, on certain conditions, predict
divergence between regions and countries in the
world economy. In this chapter I develop this
demand-oriented export-led growth model and
consider the conditions under which divergence
is likely to take place, but without imposing a
balance of payments constraint. (That is done in
Chapter 5.)

The Model

As mentioned already, the main idea behind the model is that export demand is the most important component of autonomous demand in an open economy, so that the growth of exports will govern the long-run growth of output to which other components of demand adapt. Thus we may write:

$$g_t = \gamma(x_t), \qquad (4.1)$$

where g_t is the growth of output at time t and x_t is the growth of exports. But what determines the growth of exports? We can use a conventional multiplicative (constant elasticity) export demand function which makes export demand a function of relative prices measured in a common currency (competitiveness), and income outside the country:

$$X_t = A \, (P_{dt}/P_{ft})^\eta \, Z_t^\varepsilon, \qquad (4.2)$$

so that taking rates of change (lower-case letters):

$$x_t = \eta \, (p_{dt} - p_{ft}) + \varepsilon \, (z_t), \qquad (4.3)$$

where P_d is domestic prices; P_f is competitors' prices measured in a common currency; Z is income outside the country; $\eta \; (< 0)$ is the price elasticity of demand for exports; and $\varepsilon \; (> 0)$ is the income elasticity of demand for exports.

The growth of income outside the economy and foreign prices may be taken as exogenous, but the growth of domestic prices is assumed to be endogenous, derived from a mark-up pricing equation in which prices are based on labour costs per unit of output plus a percentage mark-up:

$$P_{dt} = (W_t / R_t) (T_t), \qquad (4.4)$$

where W is the money wage rate, R is the average product of labour, and T is $1 + \%$ mark-up on unit labour costs. Taking rates of change gives:

$$p_{dt} = w_t - r_t + \tau_t. \qquad (4.5)$$

Productivity growth, however, is partly dependent on the growth of output itself through static and dynamic returns to scale: Verdoorn's Law (see Chapter 3):

$$r_t = r_{at} + \lambda (g_t), \qquad (4.6)$$

where r_{at} is autonomous productivity growth, and λ is the Verdoorn coefficient.

The Verdoorn relation opens up the possibility of a virtuous circle of export-led growth. The model becomes circular because the faster the growth of output the faster the growth of productivity; and the faster the growth of productivity the slower the growth of unit labour costs, and hence the faster the growth of exports and output. The model also implies that, once a country obtains a growth advantage, it will tend to sustain it. Suppose, for example, that an economy acquires an advantage in the production of goods with a high income elasticity of demand in world markets (technology-based activities) which raises its growth rate above that of other economies. Owing to the Verdoorn effect, productivity growth will be higher and the competitive advantage of the economy in these goods will be reinforced, making it difficult for other economies to produce the same commodities except through protection or exceptional industrial enterprise. In centre–periphery models of growth and development, it is differences between the income elasticity characteristics of exports and imports which lie at the core of the problem for the periphery and at the heart of the success of the centre (Thirlwall, 1983).

The equilibrium solution of the model is obtained by successive substitution of (4.6) into (4.5), the result into (4.3) and this into (4.1) which gives:

$$\dot{g}_t = \gamma \frac{\left[\eta \left(\dot{w}_t - r_{st} + \tau_t - p_{ft} \right) + \varepsilon \left(\dot{z}_t \right) \right]}{1 + \gamma \eta \lambda}. \qquad (4.7)$$

Remembering that $\eta < 0$, the equilibrium growth rate is shown to vary positively with autonomous productivity growth, the rate of growth of foreign prices and the growth of world income, and negatively with domestic wage growth and an increase in the mark-up. The Verdoorn coefficient (λ) serves to exaggerate growth rate differences between economies arising from differences in other parameters and variables (that is, the higher λ, the smaller the denominator, since $\eta < 0$). If $\lambda = 0$, there is no exaggeration of differences.

Now it is an interesting question whether country growth rates will tend to diverge through time. This depends on the behaviour of the model out of equilibrium. In a two-country model, a necessary condition for divergence is that the growth rate of one of the countries diverges from its own equilibrium rate. One way to consider a model in disequilibrium, and to examine its dynamics, is to put lags into the equation. If we put a one-period lag into the export growth equation (4.2), we obtain a first-order difference equation, the solution to which is:

$$g_t = A \, (- \gamma \eta \lambda)^t + \text{particular (equilibrium) solution.}$$
(4.8)

Since $\eta < 0$, $(- \gamma \eta \lambda) > 0$, so there are no cycles. If $| \gamma \eta \lambda | > 1$, there will be explosive growth as t increases. If $| \gamma \eta \lambda | < 1$, there will be convergence to equilibrium. If, for the moment, it is assumed that $\gamma = 1$, this would mean there would be cumulative divergence away from equilibrium if $| - \eta \lambda | > 1$. Given a Verdoorn coefficient of 0.5, this would imply a price elasticity of demand for exports greater than 2. This is possible.

In practice, however, it is not usual to observe growth rates between countries diverging through time. Levels of per capita income diverge, but not the growth of output. Growth rates between countries differ not because we observe countries in the process of divergence but because the equilibrium growth rates differ, associated mainly with differences in the income elasticity of demand for exports (ε). What keeps growth on its equilibrium path is likely to be a balance of payments equilibrium requirement. Typically, imports grow faster than output. This means that exports must also grow faster than output. This implies that γ in equation (4.1) will be substantially less than unity. If relative price changes are ruled out as a balance of payments adjustment mechanism, γ will be the reciprocal of the income elasticity of demand for imports. For example, if the import elasticity is 2, then $\gamma =$ 0.5. This means (from equation 4.8) that the price elasticity of demand for exports would have to be greater than 4 for divergence from equilibrium to occur. Such a high elasticity for aggregate exports is highly unusual.[1]

If the above model is simply treated as an export-led growth model with no feedback mechanism through the Verdoorn effect, and relative prices are held constant, equation (4.7) reduces to:

$$g_t = \gamma \varepsilon (z_t). \qquad (4.9)$$

If a balance of payments constraint is imposed, $\gamma = 1/\pi$, where π is the income elasticity of demand for imports. Therefore:

The nature of economic growth

$$g_t = \varepsilon \, (z_t)/\pi \qquad (4.10)$$

or

$$g_t/z_t = \varepsilon/\pi. \qquad (4.11)$$

This says that one country's growth rate relative to all others (z) is equiproportional to the ratio of the income elasticity of demand for exports and imports. I discovered this rule in 1979 (Thirlwall, 1979), which turns out to be the dynamic analogue of the static Harrod trade multiplier (Harrod, 1933) and I elaborate it and its implications more fully in the next chapter. Paul Krugman (1989) discovered it ten years later and for obvious reasons called it the 45-degree rule (relative growth rates are equiproportional to relative income elasticities). However, he reverses the direction of causation, which makes him an orthodox neoclassical economist as far as growth theory is concerned. In his model, the growth of the labour force determines output growth, and fast output growth leads to fast export growth – hence an apparently higher income elasticity of demand for exports. The direction of causation is therefore from growth to export elasticities, not from elasticities to growth. It is tautologically true, of course, that *if* faster-growing countries manage to sell more exports, they will be observed to have a higher elasticity, but the model does not explain how fast growth arises in the first place (except by the assumption of a faster growth of the labour force), or why a faster-growing country will necessarily export more independent of the characteristics of the goods it produces. Greater supply availability and/or variety is not sufficient if demand is relatively lacking.

In the final analysis, it is a question of to what extent income elasticities can be considered as exogenously determined and to what extent they are endogenously determined by the growth of output itself. In this respect, it should not be forgotten that, in many instances, countries' income elasticities are largely determined by natural resource endowments and the characteristics of the goods produced which are the product of history and independent of the growth of output. An obvious example is the contrast between primary product production and industrial production, where primary products tend to have an income elasticity of demand less than unity (Engel's Law) while most industrial products have an income elasticity greater than unity. In my model, where the direction of causation is from elasticities to growth, the elasticities reflect the *structure* of production. This is the basic assumption of all the classic centre–periphery models including those of Prebisch, Myrdal and Seers, and also Kaldor (1970). Even between industrial countries (with which Krugman is primarily concerned), feedback mechanisms of the type already described (associated with Verdoorn's Law) will tend to perpetuate initial differences in income elasticities associated with 'inferior' industrial structures on the one hand and 'superior' industrial structures on the other.

Empirical Evidence on Exports and Growth

Let us now consider the interpretation of the empirical evidence that exists on the relationship between export growth and GDP growth. There has been a massive amount of research in recent years showing a link between export and output growth (see Thirlwall, 2000 for a survey). In fact, output growth probably correlates more closely with export growth than any other variable introduced into growth equations. There is likely to be bi-directional causality through mechanisms described earlier. The *causal* mechanism by which export growth affects output growth, however, is often not specified and, where it is, it is normally a neoclassical supply-side argument. It is assumed that the export sector has a higher level of productivity than the non-export sector, and that, because of exposure to foreign competition, the export sector confers externalities on the non-export sector. Therefore both the share of exports in GDP and the growth of exports matters for overall growth performance.

Feder (1983) was the first to develop a formal model on these lines which fits neatly into mainstream neoclassical growth theory, where the conventional production function is augmented by three terms: the growth of exports, the share of exports in GDP, and a coefficient combining the differential productivity and externality effects. The equation derived is:

$$g = a(I/Y) + b(dL/L) + [\delta(1 + \delta) + F_x](X/Y)(dX/X), \tag{4.12}$$

where I/Y is the investment ratio as a proxy for capital accumulation; dL/L is the growth of the labour force; X/Y is the share of exports in GDP; dX/X is the growth of exports; $\delta(1 + \delta)$ measures the differential productivity effect between the two sectors and F_x measures the externality effect. Feder tests the model across 31 countries over the period 1964–73, first without export growth and then with. The inclusion of dX/X improves considerably the explanatory power. Then the export share term is excluded to isolate the externality effect. The difference between the total export effect on growth and the externality effect is the differential productivity effect. There is evidence of both externality and differential productivity effects.

The model certainly has plausibility, but it is a pure supply-side argument, and not the only possible one. There are other possible supply-side arguments, and also demand-side arguments, consistent with a strong correlation between export and output growth. For example, as we argued at the beginning, fast export growth permits fast import growth. Imports, particularly of capital goods and intermediate inputs, are a vehicle for the transfer of technology which can have spillover effects on output (Grossman and Helpman, 1991). Also, if countries are short of foreign exchange, and domestic and foreign resources are not fully substitutable, more imports permit a fuller use of domestic resources. Esfahani (1991) recognizes this latter point and re-estimates Feder's equation for 31 countries, including import growth as well as export growth. The export growth variable now loses its significance, while the import growth variable is significant. The regression equation is also run without export growth, and it is found that, once the import supply-side effect of exports is taken into account, there is apparently no significant externality effect of exports left to explain. Esfahani concludes, 'even though exports do not appear to have had much direct external-ity effect on GDP – export promotion policies in these countries can be quite valuable in supplying foreign exchange which relieves import shortages and permits output expansion'.

But even the Esfahani argument does not go far enough because, as argued at the beginning, there are equally (if not more) important demand-side considerations to take into account which would also be consistent with finding a positive relation between export growth and GDP growth, but these considerations are rarely articulated in the mainstream trade and growth literature. Spe-cifically, export growth is a major component of aggregate demand, and may set up a virtuous circle of growth. But even more important, in most developing countries at least, the major constraint on the growth of demand is the current balance of payments and a shortage of foreign exchange. Export growth relaxes this constraint and is unique in allowing all other components of demand to grow faster without balance of payments difficulties arising. This is the simplest of all explanations of the relationship between export and output growth, and leads on to the modelling of balance of payments constrained growth models.

Note

1. Recently, more sophisticated models of cumulative causation have been developed (for example, Leon-Ledesma, 2000b) containing elements of both divergence and convergence. Specifically, the export growth equation is augmented to include a technology variable which depends on cumulative output, education and the productivity gap between a country and the technological leader. The productivity growth equation also depends on the level of technology and the technological gap. Whether there is divergence or convergence becomes an empirical matter depending on the parameter values of the model.

5. Balance of payments constrained growth: theory and evidence

It has been a central feature of most of my own work on growth to try and put demand back into growth theory, and to argue that for most countries demand constraints bite long before supply constraints operate, and that, to understand growth rate differences between countries over the long run, the analysis and understanding of demand constraints cannot be ignored. In an open economy, the major constraint on the growth of demand (and therefore growth performance) is likely to be its balance of payments. At a theoretical level, it can be stated as a fundamental proposition that no country can grow faster than that rate consistent with balance of payments equilibrium on current account unless it can finance ever-growing deficits, which, in general, it cannot. There is a limit to the deficit to GDP ratio (Moreno Brid, 1998), and a limit to the debt to GDP ratio beyond which the financial markets become nervous and a country is unable to borrow more. If capital flows are included in the model, every country must have a growth rate consistent with its overall balance of payments because, by definition, the total balance of payments must balance.

At the empirical (observational) level, the evidence for the proposition I am making is that many countries find themselves in balance of payments difficulties, and have to constrain growth, while the economy still has surplus capacity and surplus labour. There are certainly not many developing countries in the world that could not grow faster given the greater availability of foreign exchange. Obviously, not every country in the world can be balance of payments constrained simultaneously, since the world itself is a closed trading system, but it only requires one country or group of countries not to be constrained for all the rest to be so. Constrainers in the past have been countries such as Japan, Germany, Switzerland and many of the oil-producing countries of the Middle East. Keynes at Bretton Woods recognized the deflationary consequences of persistent balance of payments surpluses, and would have penalized surplus countries in the same way that deficit countries are penalized, but his proposal was rejected (see Thirlwall, 1987b, where the Keynes Plan 'Proposals for an International Clearing Union' is reprinted).

Below, I develop a model of balance of payments constrained growth, first without capital flows, and then including capital flows. I will then discuss tests of the model, and examine some of the more recent empirical evidence. The inspiration for developing this class of model came in the 1970s when I was working with a PhD student (R.J. Dixon) on *regional* export-led growth models (of the type outlined in Chapter 4), but where balance of payments problems are not apparent in the normal sense of regions within a country having to defend an exchange rate, since they are part of a common currency area. It occurred to me, however, that in these regional export-led growth models, when applied to countries, it cannot be assumed that there are no demand constraints at all. Suppose, for example, that the growth rate determined by the parameters of the model (as in equation (4.7)) leads to a faster growth of imports than exports. The growth rate would not be sustainable. In other words, imports need modelling in export-led growth models, and the obvious approach is to model starting with the condition of current account equilibrium.

The Model

The structure of the model is very simple. We start with the balance of payments equilibrium condition. We then specify export and import demand functions (as in Chapter 4). Since import growth is a function of income growth, we can then solve for the growth of income consistent with balance of payments equilibrium.

Current account equilibrium is given by:

$$P_d X = P_f M E \qquad (5.1)$$

where X is the quantity of exports; P_d is the price of exports in domestic currency; M is the quantity of imports; P_f is the price of imports in foreign currency, and E is the exchange rate measured as the domestic price of foreign currency. Taking rates of growth gives:

$$p_d + x = p_f + m + e. \qquad (5.2)$$

The growth of exports (as in Chapter 4, but with the exchange rate included) is given as:

$$x = \eta \, (p_d - p_f - e) + \varepsilon \, (z). \qquad (5.3)$$

But now imports need modelling. The import demand function may be specified in the same way as the export demand function: as a multiplicative (constant elasticity) function in which imports are related to competitiveness and to domestic income as a proxy for expenditure. Thus:

$$M = B \, (P_f E / P_d)^{\psi} \, Y^{\pi}, \qquad (5.4)$$

where ψ (< 0) is the price elasticity of demand for imports; Y is domestic income, and π (> 0) is the income elasticity of demand for imports. Taking rates of change gives:

$$m = \psi \, (p_f + e - p_d) + \pi \, (y). \qquad (5.5)$$

Substituting equations (5.3) and (5.5) into (5.2) gives the rate of growth of income consistent with balance of payments equilibrium (y_B):

$$y_B = [(1 + \eta + \psi)\,(p_d - p_f - e) + \varepsilon z]/\pi. \quad (5.6)$$

Equation (5.6) expresses a number of interesting and familiar economic propositions:

1. an improvement in the real terms of trade, $(p_d - p_f - e) > 0$, will improve a country's growth rate consistent with balance of payments equilibrium. This is the pure terms of trade effect on real income growth;
2. one country's prices rising faster than another measured in a common currency will lower a country's balance of payments equilibrium growth rate if the sum of the (negative) price elasticities is greater than unity: that is $(1 + \eta + \psi) < 0$;
3. currency depreciation ($e > 0$) will raise the balance of payments equilibrium growth rate if the sum of the price elasticities is greater than unity. This is the dynamic analogue of the static Marshall–Lerner condition for an improvement in the balance of payments following currency depreciation. Note, however, that a once-for-all depreciation or devaluation of the currency cannot put a country on a *permanently* higher growth path consistent with balance of payments equilibrium since in the period after the devaluation $e = 0$, and the growth rate

would revert to its former level. Using constant
elasticity demand functions, the currency depreciation would have to be continuous, but this
would soon feed through to domestic prices,
nullifying the exchange rate advantage;

4. the equation shows the mutual interdependence
   of countries because one country's growth performance (y) is linked to all others (z). But how
   fast one country can grow relative to all others,
   while preserving its balance of payments,
   depends crucially on ε, the income elasticity
   of demand for exports. For some countries, ε is
   very high (in the range 3 to 4); in other countries
   it is very low (less than unity);

5. the balance of payments equilibrium growth
   rate is inversely related to its appetite for
   imports, measured by π.

If it is now assumed that relative prices measured
in a common currency remain unchanged, equation
(5.6) reduces to:

$$y_B = \varepsilon\,(z)\,/\,\pi = x\,/\,\pi. \qquad (5.7)$$

This is the dynamic analogue of the static Harrod
trade multiplier result $Y = X/m$ (where Y is the
level of income, X is the *level* of exports and m is
the marginal propensity to import), which Harrod
derived in his book *International Economics* in
1933 on the same assumptions as above, namely
balance of payments equilibrium and no change
in the real terms of trade. I had not read Harrod

before I derived the result in equation (5.7), but when I did I realized I had reinvented the wheel, although it should be emphasized that Harrod never derived the growth implications of his result. The Harrod trade multiplier of $1/m$ was eclipsed by the closed economy Keynesian multiplier of $1/s$ (where s is the propensity to save), but in the open economy it is probably more difficult to plug an import–export gap than it is to bridge a savings–investment gap and therefore the foreign trade multiplier has more relevance for understanding the macroeconomic performance of countries. If relative prices do not adjust in international trade, or trade flows are relatively insensitive to price changes, it is output and growth that adjust to bring imports and exports into line.

The test of this model is to see how close the long run growth of countries approximates to the predicted growth rate x/π. If it is equal, or slightly above with countries running deficits, and there exist unemployed domestic resources, this is pretty convincing evidence (to me at least) that growth is balance of payments constrained. When I first applied this simple model in 1979 to a series of developed countries, I did not perform any formal parametric tests. I simply observed how close the *actual* growth rate was to the *predicted* rate and estimated rank correlations. The actual and predicted rates were remarkably close, and I rather pompously remarked, 'it might almost be stated as a fundamental law that – the rate of growth of a country will approximate to the ratio of its rate of growth of exports and its income elasticity of demand for imports. The approximation itself vindicates the assumptions used to arrive at the simple rule'. Ever since, this result has come to be known in the literature as Thirlwall's Law: not as powerful as $e = mc^2$(!), but a powerful predictor, nonetheless, of inter-country growth performance (for surveys, see *Journal of Post Keynesian Economics*, 1997, and McCombie and Thirlwall, 1997).

There are parametric tests of the model. The two main ones are as follows. The first is to run a regression of actual growth (y) on y_B for a series of countries and test whether the constant term is zero and the regression coefficient is equal to unity. If so, y_B will be a good predictor of y. This test has been performed by some investigators with mixed results, but there are at least two major problems with the test. The first is that there will be bias if a sample of countries is taken in which the balance of payments deficits and surpluses do not cancel out: that is, if there is a systematic tendency for $y > y_B$ or $y < y_B$. Secondly, there may well be outliers where $y \neq y_B$ (for example, Japan) which gives a regression coefficient significantly different from unity, leading to a rejection of the theory for all other countries.

A second (alternative) test which avoids the above problems is to take each country separately and to estimate the income elasticity of demand for imports (say π') that would make $y = y_B$, and then to compare this with the estimated π from time series regression analysis of the import demand function. If π' is not significantly different from π, y and y_B will not differ significantly either. When this test is done, the model is supported in the vast majority of cases. The cases where it is not are typically countries that have run either large balance of payments surpluses for a long period of time, or large deficits financed by capital inflows. This leads on to the extension of the basic model to include the capital account of the balance of payments.

The Model with Capital Flows

With capital flows, equation (5.1) becomes:

$$P_d X + C = P_f M E \tag{5.8}$$

where $C > 0$ is capital inflows measured in domestic currency. This is an identity because the balance of payments must balance in total. Taking rates of change of (5.8), and substituting (5.3) and (5.5), gives the rate of growth of income consistent with the *total* balance of payments:

$$y_{BT} = [(p_d - p_f - e) + (\theta\eta + \psi)(p_d - p_f - e) + \theta \varepsilon z \\ + (1 - \theta)(c - p_d)] / \pi, \tag{5.9}$$

where c is the growth of nominal capital inflows; θ is the share of exports in total receipts to pay for imports, and $(1 - \theta)$ is the share of capital inflows in total receipts. The first term in equation (5.9) gives the pure terms of trade effect on real income growth. The second term gives the volume effect of relative price changes. The third term gives the effect of exogenous changes in income growth abroad, and the fourth term gives the effect of the growth of *real* capital inflows which 'finance' growth in excess of the rate of growth consistent with equilibrium on current account.

Since equation (5.9) is derived from an identity, it is possible to disaggregate any country's growth rate into the above four components, and to compare countries or groups of countries. One of the latest studies to do this is by Nureldin-Hussain (1999). He takes a sample of 29 African countries which grew on average at 3.66 per cent per annum and 11 Asian countries which grew on average at 6.60 per cent, and analyses differences between them in terms of equation (5.9). There is not much difference between the two sets of countries as far as terms of trade movements are concerned. The effect of capital inflows on growth is slightly lower in Asia than in Africa. The big difference comes through the growth in the volume of exports which in Asia gives a growth rate of 5.91 per cent while in Africa it produces a growth rate of only 2.45 per cent – less than half. This highlights once again the importance of differences in the structure of production and income elasticities of demand for exports in contributing to differences in growth performance between countries. Africa is still dominated by the export of primary products, while Asia has diversified into manufactures.

Policy Implications

The simple policy implication for most countries is that, if they wish to grow faster, they must first raise the balance of payments constraint on demand. The challenge for economic policy-making is how to do this effectively. The IMF prescription is normally liberalization and currency depreciation. While trade liberalization may improve export performance, it may also lead to a faster growth of imports which worsens the balance of payments (see Santos-Paulino and Thirlwall, 2001). Among international organizations, only UNCTAD (1999) seems to recognize this possibility. Liberalization of the capital account of the balance of payments is also fraught with problems without internal macroeconomic stability. Domestic interest rates which are too high will lead to capital inflows and overvalued currencies which damage the tradeable goods sector. Equally, domestic crisis may lead to rapid capital outflows, depreciating the currency excessively, leading to inflation.

As far as devaluation is concerned, we have shown that currency depreciation cannot raise a country's growth rate on a permanent basis unless it is continuous, or it changes favourably other parameters of the model. The exchange rate, however, is not an efficient instrument for structural change because it simply makes countries more competitive (temporarily) in the goods that cause the balance of payments problems in the first place. Countries can try and make their goods more price-competitive by other means, but many of the goods developing countries produce (at least collectively) are price inelastic (for example, primary commodities). It is the non-price characteristics of goods such as their quality, technical sophistication and marketing which seem to be the most important factor in determining trade performance.

Countries can impose import controls to reduce the income elasticity of demand for imports (π) but this can breed serious inefficiency. It is true, however, and worth remembering in debates over protection, that no country in the world, apart from the United Kingdom, has ever industrialized without protection of one form or another. Export promotion and import substitution are not incompatible strategies, as Japan and South Korea have demonstrated in the post-war years. The distinguished development economist Ajit Singh tells how, when he first went to Cambridge to study economics, Nicholas Kaldor taught him three things: first, the only way for a country to develop is to industrialize; second, the only way for a country to industrialize is to protect itself; and third, anyone who says otherwise is being dishonest! The developed economies do preach double standards. They preach free trade for developing countries, yet protect their own markets. There is an economic case for protection to alter the structure of production and to improve the balance of payments, but it needs to be implemented with prudence and skill to avoid the protection of high-cost inefficient industries and the pursuit of rent seeking.

Countries can encourage greater capital inflows to finance import growth in excess of export growth, but care needs to be taken with the type of capital inflow. Long-term direct investment is probably the most stable and beneficial, but foreign investment can also cause problems relating to the nature of the goods produced, the techniques of production employed and the outflow of profits. Most other types of inflow, apart from pure aid, involve debt-service repayments, and debt problems can arise if the inflows are not translated into improved export performance which earn the foreign exchange to pay interest and amortization. Even if the borrowing is invested in the tradeable goods sector, foreign exchange is not guaranteed because the growth of exports is outside the control of the countries concerned. The export growth of developing countries depends largely on the health of the world economy, which became dramatically apparent during the debt crisis of the early 1980s.

The only sure and long-term solution to raising a country's growth rate consistent with balance of payments equilibrium on current account is structural change to raise ε and to reduce π. We are back to the ideas of Raul Prebisch and the question of the most appropriate industrial policy for countries, and the role of protection.

6. The endogeneity of the natural rate of growth

It was Harrod who first formally introduced the concept of the natural rate of growth into economic theory in his paper, 'An Essay in Dynamic Theory' (Harrod, 1939), which was discussed in Chapter 1. The natural rate of growth refers to the rate of growth of productive potential of an economy, or the 'social optimum' rate of growth, as Harrod called it. In all of mainstream growth theory, the natural rate of growth (composed of labour force growth and labour productivity growth) is treated as *exogenously* determined, unresponsive to the actual rate of growth or the pressure of demand in an economy. It is exogenous in Harrod's original model, which is why Harrod's growth model is not really a growth model at all, but a trade cycle model, because it does not explain growth. It is treated as exogenous in the neoclassical response to Harrod, as in the original model of Solow (1956), for example, as discussed in Chapter 2. It is treated as exogenous (by and large) in the post-Keynesian response to the neoclassicals, as in the original models of Kaldor (1957) and Joan Robinson (1956). Paradoxically, it is even treated as exogenous in 'new' *endogenous* growth theory. In 'new' growth theory, growth is endogenous in the sense that investment matters for growth, because the assumption of diminishing returns to capital is relaxed, not in the sense that labour force growth and productivity growth respond to demand and the growth of output itself. Demand is entirely missing from 'new' endogenous growth theory.

Then, when it comes to empirical studies of growth rate differences between countries, we find that exogeneity of factor supplies and productivity growth permeates the whole of the mainstream literature on the sources of growth, as in the pioneer studies of Abramovitz (1956), Solow (1957), Denison (1967) and Maddison (1970) among others, and the recent work of Alwyn Young (1995) on South East Asia and Hu and Khan (1997) on China, as discussed in Chapter 2.

But the question arises, suppose the natural rate of growth, or a country's growth of productive potential, is not exogenous, but endogenous to demand or the actual rate of growth? What implications does this have? It has two major implications. First, at the theoretical level, it has implications for the efficiency and speed of the adjustment process between the warranted and natural rates of growth in the Harrod model. Secondly, and more important, it has implications for the way we view the growth process, and why growth rates differ between countries: whether we view growth as supply-determined, or whether we view growth as demand-determined or determined by constraints on demand before supply constraints become operative. The view taken here is that it is a mistake to think of the natural rate of growth as exogenously determined. In other words, there is nothing natural about the natural rate of growth, just as there is nothing natural about the natural rate of unemployment (but that is another story). Both the growth of the labour force and productivity growth are positively related to demand or the actual rate of growth.

The view that growth is primarily demand-driven, to which supply responds, does not mean, of course, that demand growth determines supply growth without limit; rather, that aggregate demand determines aggregate supply over a range of full employment growth rates, and that in most countries demand constraints tend to bite long before supply constraints are ever reached.

Later, I will suggest a simple technique for testing the endogeneity of the natural rate of growth and give some empirical results for a sample of 15 OECD countries over the period 1961 to 1995. First, however, let us discuss the theoretical consequences of the natural rate being endogenous.

Although it was Harrod in 1939 who first coined the term 'the natural rate of growth', as a matter of historical interest, Keynes had effectively anticipated Harrod's idea two years earlier in his Galton Lecture to the Eugenics Society in 1937 on 'Some Economic Consequences of a Declining

Population' (Keynes, 1937), where he expressed the worry that, because of a falling population, there would not be enough demand to absorb full employment saving. Consider, he says, an economy with a savings ratio of 8–15 per cent of national income, and a capital–output ratio of 4, giving a rate of capital accumulation which will absorb saving of approximately 2–4 per cent. With a constant capital–output ratio, this is the required growth of output, but can this rate be guaranteed? Historically, it appeared to Keynes that one-half of the increase in capital accumulation (or demand for investment) could be attributed to increased population; the other half to increased living standards (productivity growth). Now suppose population growth falls to zero. Since the standard of life cannot be expected to grow by more than 1 per cent per annum, this means that the demand for capital will only grow at 1 per cent while the supply grows at between 2 and 4 per cent – a clear and worrying imbalance which would have to be rectified either by reducing saving or by reducing the rate of interest to lengthen the average period of production (that is, to raise the capital–output ratio). This discussion is exactly analogous to Harrod's discussion of divergence between the warranted and natural rates of growth. The required rate of growth to absorb saving is the warranted rate of growth, and the long-run growth rate determined by population (labour force) growth and rising living standards (productivity growth through technical progress) is the natural rate of growth. Harrod's dynamic theory is precisely anticipated by Keynes; and Keynes, like Harrod, treats the natural growth rate as exogenous.

Given the definition of the natural rate of growth as the sum of the rate of growth of the labour force and the rate of growth of labour productivity, it follows that the measured natural rate must be that rate of growth that keeps the unemployment rate constant. Otherwise, if the actual growth rate is above the natural rate, the unemployment rate will fall; and if the actual growth rate is below the natural rate, the unemployment rate will rise. For the purposes here, I define and measure the natural growth rate of countries as the rate which keeps the rate of unemployment constant.

The natural growth rate fulfils two functions in the Harrod model. Firstly, it sets the ceiling to the divergence between the actual and warranted growth rates and turns cyclical booms into slumps. Secondly, as implied earlier, it gives the long-run potential growth rate to which economies might gravitate given the right conditions. But there was no mechanism in the original Harrod model to bring the warranted and natural rates of growth in line with one another, with the consequence that economies might experience perpetual secular stagnation (if the warranted rate exceeds the natural rate) or permanent inflation and structural unemployment (if the natural rate exceeds the warranted rate, as in most developing countries where population growth is high and savings low). Mechanisms that might achieve equilibrium, however, were soon invented. The Cambridge, Massachusetts school, represented by Robert Solow, Paul Samuelson and Franco Modigliani, used the neoclassical production function and variations in the capital–output ratio to show that the warranted growth rate would adjust to the natural rate (assuming, of course, appropriate factor price adjustment and a spectrum of production techniques to choose from). The Cambridge, England school, represented by Nicholas Kaldor, Joan Robinson, Richard Kahn and Luigi Pasinetti, used variations in the savings ratio brought about by changes in the functional distribution of income between wages and profits as the mechanism to bring about equilibrium. But both schools have equilibrium growth proceeding at the *exogenously* given natural rate.

What happens, however, if the natural rate of growth is not exogenous? This has interesting consequences both for the short-run trade cycle model of Harrod and for the long-run equilibrium growth model. Recall that, in the trade cycle model (see Chapter 1), if the actual growth rate diverges from the warranted growth rate in either direction, forces come into play which widen the divergence – but divergence is bounded by ceilings and floors. The ceiling is the natural rate of growth because the level of output cannot exceed the full employment ceiling. But suppose the natural rate increases with the actual rate of growth (because labour force growth and productivity growth are induced); this will perpetuate the cyclical upturn. One interesting conjecture is that this increases the possibility that the cyclical upturn is not brought to an end by an absolute ceiling, but by demand constraints associated with inflation and balance of payments problems due to bottlenecks in the system. This may explain why cyclical peaks are often accompanied by excess capacity. In any case, the endogeneity of the natural rate will surely lengthen the cycle.

In the long-period model of divergence between the warranted and natural growth rate, the endogeneity of the natural rate will impede adjustment to equilibrium. If the warranted rate exceeds the natural rate, it means that the growth of capital exceeds the growth of the labour force in efficiency units and the warranted rate must fall for equilibrium. In conditions of recession, however, the natural rate is also likely to fall as workers leave the labour force and productivity growth slows, impeding adjustment. Similarly, if the natural rate exceeds the warranted rate, this implies that the growth of the effective labour force exceeds the growth of capital and the warranted rate must rise for equilibrium. In booms, however, the natural rate is also likely to rise as workers are attracted into the labour force and productivity growth accelerates, also impeding adjustment.

In general, the endogeneity of the natural rate of growth has serious implications for the notion of a *given* full employment production frontier which economies will gravitate towards. In practice, the frontier will continually shift with the actual growth rate.

In What Ways is the Natural Rate Endogenous?

There are many mechanisms through which the natural rate of growth is likely to be endogenous to the actual rate of growth. Consider first the growth of the labour force or labour supply. Labour supply is extremely elastic to demand. When the demand for labour is strong, labour input responds in a number of ways. Firstly, participation rates rise. Workers previously out of the labour force decide to join the labour force. The participation rates of the young, the old, and married women are particularly flexible. Secondly, hours worked increase. Part-time workers become full-time workers, and overtime work increases. Thirdly, and significantly for many countries across the world, labour migration takes place in response to booming labour markets. If countries are short of labour, they import it. Cornwall (1977) and Kindleberger (1967) document the important role that immigrant labour played in Europe during the 'golden age' of economic growth between 1950 and 1973. The migration of labour from Portugal, Spain, Greece and Turkey into Germany, France, Switzerland and northern Italy was not an exogenous movement but was fuelled by an excess demand for labour in the receiving countries because the growth of demand for output was so high (largely due to rapid export growth). Similar stories could be told for other parts of the world.

Now consider the growth of labour productivity. There are several mechanisms through which labour productivity growth is endogenous to demand, and well documented. First, there are static and dynamic returns to scale associated with increases in the volume of output and the technical progress incorporated in capital accumulation. Some technical progress is autonomous, but a great deal is demand-driven, particularly process innovation. Necessity is the mother of invention! Secondly, there are macro increasing returns in the Allyn Young (1928) sense associated with the inter-related expansion of all activities. If the market for a good expands, it makes it profitable to use more sophisticated machinery, which cuts costs. This not only reduces the price of the good (leading to further expansion of demand) but will also reduce the price of machinery if there are economies of scale in its production which makes it profitable to use machinery in other activities. The initial demand expansion leads to a series of changes which propagate themselves in a cumulative way, causing labour productivity to rise. Thirdly, there is the well known phenomenon of learning by doing whereby the efficiency or productivity of labour is an increasing function of a learning process related to cumulative output. The more output produced, the more adept labour becomes at producing it. Clearly, the impact of learning will gradually diminish with successive amounts of the same output, but as long as product ranges change over time, the effect of learning on productivity growth will be a continuous process related to the expansion of output. All the phenomena mentioned above are captured by the Verdoorn relation, or Verdoorn's Law, discussed in Chapter 3. Given this relationship between the growth of output and induced productivity growth, it is no accident that, when growth slows down, productivity growth also slows down. The productivity growth slowdown after the shocks to the world economy in the 1970s was regarded as a puzzle by some economists, but can be readily understood in the context of models in which productivity growth is endogenous.

Estimating the Natural Rate and Testing its Endogeneity

Let us now turn to the question of how the natural rate of growth of a country may be estimated, and to test whether it is endogenous. Many years ago (Thirlwall, 1969), I suggested a simple technique for estimating the natural rate of growth based on a modification of the equations used for testing Okun's Law (Okun, 1962) relating to the relation between changes in unemployment and the gap between actual and potential output. We saw earlier that, by definition, the natural rate must be the growth rate which keeps the rate of unemployment constant. If we therefore relate changes in unemployment in a country to its growth rate, we can solve for the growth of output that keeps unemployment constant. In other words, let

$$\Delta\% \; U = a - b \, (g), \qquad (6.1)$$

where $\% \; U$ is the percentage rate of unemployment and g is the growth rate. Solving for g when $\Delta\% \; U = 0$ gives an expression for the natural rate of growth of $g_n = a/b$. The technique is simple, but there are certain problems. The estimate of the coefficient 'b' may be biased downwards because of labour hoarding which would exaggerate the estimate of g_n. Equally, however, the constant term 'a' may be biased downwards through workers leaving the labour force where g is low, depressing the estimate of g_n. It is difficult to know *a priori* what the relative strengths of the (offsetting) biases are likely to be.

An alternative procedure is to reverse the variables in equation (6.1) to give:

$$g = a_1 - b_1 \, (\Delta\% \; U). \qquad (6.2)$$

Solving for g when $\Delta\% \; U = 0$ now gives an estimate for the natural rate of growth of $g_n = a_1$. This also has statistical problems since the change in unemployment is an endogenous variable, although it transpires empirically that this does not affect the results obtained from fitting (6.2). Originally, I tested both ways for the United States and the United Kingdom using (6.1) and (6.2) and obtained the same results for the period 1950 to

1967: a natural rate for the UK of 2.9 per cent and for the US of 3.3 per cent, which seemed eminently reasonable estimates.

To my knowledge, the technique has not been used subsequently, but if this simple way of estimating the natural rate of growth is accepted, the obvious way to test for endogeneity is to include a dummy variable into (say) equation (6.2) in periods when the actual growth rate is above the estimated natural rate and test for its significance:

$$g = a_2 + b_2 D - c_2 \, (\Delta\% \; U), \qquad (6.3)$$

where D takes the value of 1 when actual growth is greater than the natural rate and zero otherwise. If the dummy is significant, this must mean that the rate of growth in periods of boom to keep unemployment constant has risen. The actual growth rate must have been pulling more workers into the labour force and inducing productivity growth. The constant term 'a_2' plus b_2 gives the natural rate of growth in boom periods. The interesting question is then how this estimate of the natural rate in boom periods compares with the estimate of the natural rate which does not distinguish between boom and slump. What is the elasticity of the natural rate in periods of boom?

The procedures described above can be illustrated by means of a simple diagram (Figure 6.1). The growth of output is measured on the vertical axis and the change in the percentage level of unemployment on the horizontal axis. The scatter

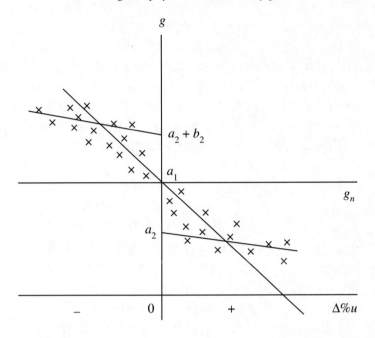

Figure 6.1

points relate to the time series relation between the two variables. Since the natural rate of growth is defined as that rate which keeps unemployment constant, a_1 is the estimated natural rate over the whole sample period not distinguishing between periods of boom and slump. If we then distinguish between periods when $g > g_n$ and $g < g_n$, the question is whether the intercept differs, or do they share the common intercept a_1? Note that in practice not all observations will lie where they should theoretically in the top left and bottom right quadrants of the diagram (with $\Delta\% U > 0$ when $g < g_n$ and $\Delta\% U < 0$ when

$g > g_n$) because the relation between g and $\Delta\%$ U is stochastic. Some observations may lie in the top right and bottom left quadrants, which could bias estimates of the intercepts between the two regimes. This is tested for, and it is found that 'rogue' observations make no statistical difference to the results to be presented below.

Empirical Results

To test the model, a sample of 15 OECD countries is taken over the period 1961 to 1995. Both equations (6.1) and (6.2) were fitted to estimate the natural rate of growth over the whole period. In general, equation (6.2) gave the best results in terms of goodness of fit of the equations and the reasonableness of the results. In equation (6.2), the estimate of the natural rate of growth is given by the constant term (a_1), and this is reported for all countries in the first column of Table 6.1. The constant term was estimated as statistically significant in all 15 countries. The estimates of the natural rate all look reasonable for the countries concerned, and range from 2.5 per cent in the UK (the lowest) to 4.6 per cent in Japan (the highest). The average natural growth rate for the 15 OECD countries as a whole is 3.5 per cent.

When a dummy variable was added to equation (6.2) for years when the actual growth rate exceeded the estimated natural rate (equation 6.3), it was found to be significant in all 15 countries. The sum of the dummy plus the new constant

(a_2) gives the natural rate in boom periods, and is shown in column 2 of Table 6.1. The natural rate is seen to increase considerably in all countries, but in some countries by more than others. Taking the countries as a whole, the average increase is 1.8 percentage points, which is to say that the actual rate of growth in boom periods has induced labour force growth and productivity growth by that amount. The countries where the sensitivity of the natural rate seems to be greatest are those where the reserves of labour are known to be highest, such as Greece and Italy (due to surplus labour in the south), and where output growth has induced impressive technical progress through learning and sectoral rationalization, such as Japan. In general, the results show substantial elasticity of the labour force and productivity growth with respect to the pressure of demand in the economy, and it is important to stress that these results are not measuring simply the *cyclical* effect of demand on output growth because this is captured by the coefficient, c_2, in equation (6.3). The results are capturing the longer-lasting effects that sustained demand expansion has had on the growth of productive potential over the cycle.

Conclusion

The conclusion to this chapter can provide a fitting conclusion to the book as a whole. In mainstream growth theory, including 'new' growth theory, the natural rate of growth is treated as exogenously

Table 6.1 Sensitivity of the natural rate of growth to the actual rate of growth

Country	Natural rate (%) (1)	Natural rate in boom periods (%) (2)	Increase in natural rate in boom periods	
			Absolute difference (2)–(1)	Increase (%)
Australia	3.9985	5.7131	1.7146	42.9
Austria	3.1358	4.9563	1.8205	58.1
Belgium	3.5239	4.9102	1.3863	39.3
Canada	3.8352	5.2613	1.4261	37.2
Denmark	2.9424	4.7826	1.8402	62.5
France	2.8270	3.9343	1.1073	39.2
Germany	3.5054	4.7091	1.2037	34.3
Greece	4.5089	7.6711	3.1622	70.1
Italy	3.3439	5.9104	2.5665	76.8
Japan	4.5671	8.7199	4.1528	90.9
Netherlands	3.2817	5.3151	2.0334	62.0
Norway	3.9722	5.0094	1.0372	26.1
Spain	4.0623	6.0928	2.0305	50.0
UK	2.5438	3.8022	1.2584	49.5
USA	2.9911	3.6642	0.6731	22.5
Average	3.5359	5.3634	1.8275	51.7

determined, unrelated to demand or the actual rate of growth. If supply or output potential responds to demand, however, this raises the crucial question, what does it mean to say that output growth is supply-determined, or constrained by supply? Of course, it is true in a trivial sense that capital and labour are required to produce output, and how much output is produced will also depend on the level of technical efficiency, but the really important question is, why does the growth of capital, and technical progress, differ so much between countries? The supply-oriented, neoclassical production function approach to the analysis of growth cannot answer this question, and for the most part never asks it!

What has been shown in this last chapter is that it is a mistake to regard the natural rate of growth as exogenously given. The rate of growth necessary to keep the percentage level of unemployment constant rises in boom periods and falls in recession because the labour force and productivity growth are elastic to demand and output growth. This is also confirmed using causality tests between input and output growth (not reported here, but see Leon-Ledesma and Thirlwall, 2002). The orthodox and 'new' growth theories that assume that it is input growth that *unidirectionally* causes output growth finds no support from the evidence. The implication for growth theory and policy is that it makes little economic sense to think of growth as supply-constrained if demand, within limits, creates its own supply. If factor inputs (including productivity growth) react endogenously, the process of growth, and growth rate difference between countries, can only be properly understood in terms of differences in the strength of demand, and constraints on demand. For most countries, and particularly developing

countries, demand constraints operate long before
capacity is reached. Demand constraints are likely
to be related to supply bottlenecks which cause
inflation and balance of payments difficulties for
countries. It is this aspect of supply, and not the
growth of inputs in a production function, that
should be the main focus of enquiry in any supply-
oriented theory of economic growth.

Bibliography

M. Abramovitz (1956), Resource and Output Trends in the United States since 1870, *American Economic Review Papers and Proceedings*, May.

K. Arrow (1962), The Economic Implications of Learning by Doing, *Review of Economic Studies*, June.

R. Barro (1991), Economic Growth in a Cross Section of Countries, *Quarterly Journal of Economics*, May.

W. Baumol (1986), Productivity Growth, Convergence and Welfare, *American Economic Review*, December.

J. Cornwall (1977), *Modern Capitalism: Its Growth and Transformation* (London: Martin Robertson).

E. Denison (1962), *The Sources of Economic Growth in the US and the Alternatives before Us* (New York: Committee for Economic Development, Library of Congress).

E. Denison (1967), *Why Growth Rates Differ: Post-war Experience in Nine Western Countries* (Washington, DC: Brookings Institution).

E. Domar (1947), Expansion and Employment, *American Economic Review*, March.

A. Emmanuel (1972), *Unequal Exchange: A Study of the Imperialism of Trade* (New York: Monthly Review Press).

H. Esfahani (1991), Exports, Imports and Economic Growth in Semi-Industrialised Countries, *Journal of Development Economics*, January.

G. Feder (1983), On Exports and Economic Growth, *Journal of Development Economics*, February/April.

J. Felipe (1999), Total Factor Productivity Growth in East Asia: A Critical Survey, *Journal of Development Studies*, April.

B. Fingleton and J. McCombie (1998), Increasing Returns and Economic Growth: Some Evidence from the European Union Regions, *Oxford Economic Papers*, January

G. Frank (1967), *Capitalism and Underdevelopment in Latin America* (New York: Monthly Review Press).

Z. Griliches (1958), Research Costs and Social Returns: Hybrid Corn and Related Innovations, *Journal of Political Economy*, October.

G. Grossman and E. Helpman (1991), *Innovation and Growth in the Global Economy* (Cambridge, Mass.: MIT Press).

J.D. Hansen and J. Zhang (1996), A Kaldorian Approach to Regional Economic Growth in China, *Applied Economics*, June.

R. Harrod (1933), *International Economics* (Cambridge: Cambridge University Press).

R. Harrod (1939), An Essay in Dynamic Theory, *Economic Journal*, March.

J. Hicks (1950), *The Trade Cycle* (Oxford: Clarendon Press).

A. Hirschman (1958), *Strategy of Economic Development* (New Haven: Yale University Press).

Z.F. Hu and M.S. Khan (1997), Why is China Growing so Fast?, *IMF Staff Papers*, March.

K. Hussein and A.P. Thirlwall (2000), The AK Model of 'New' Growth Theory is the Harrod–Domar Growth Equation: Investment and Growth Revisited, *Journal of Post Keynesian Economics*, Spring.

Journal of Post Keynesian Economics (1997), Symposium on Thirlwall's Law, Spring.

N. Kaldor (1957), A Model of Economic Growth, *Economic Journal*, December.

N. Kaldor (1966), *Causes of the Slow Rate of Economic Growth of the United Kingdom* (Cambridge: Cambridge University Press).

N. Kaldor (1967), *Strategic Factors in Economic Development* (New York, Ithaca: New York State School of Industrial and Labour Relations, Cornell University).

N. Kaldor (1970), The Case for Regional Policies, *Scottish Journal of Political Economy*, November.

N. Kaldor (1972), 'Advanced Technology in a Strategy for Development: Some Lessons from Britain's Experience', in *Automation and Developing Countries* (Geneva: ILO).

N. Kaldor (1985), *Economics without Equilibrium* (Cardiff: University College Cardiff Press).

N. Kaldor (1996), *Causes of Growth and Stagnation in the World Economy* (The Raffaele Mattioli Lectures), (Cambridge: Cambridge University Press).

J.M. Keynes (1937), Some Economic Consequences of a Declining Population, *Eugenics Review*, April.

C. Kindleberger (1967), *Europe's Postwar Growth: the Role of the Labour Supply* (Cambridge, Mass.: Harvard University Press).

P. Krugman (1989), Differences in Income Elasticities and Trends in Real Exchange Rates, *European Economic Review*, May.

H. Leibenstein (1957), *Economic Backwardness and Economic Growth* (New York: Wiley).

M. Leon-Ledesma (2000a), Economic Growth and Verdoorn's Law in the Spanish Regions 1962–91, *International Review of Applied Economics*, January.

M. Leon-Ledesma (2000b), Accumulation, Innovation and Catching-Up: an Extended Cumulative Growth Model, *Cambridge Journal of Economics* , May.

M. Leon-Ledesma and A.P. Thirlwall (2002), The Endogeneity of the Natural Rate of Growth, *Cambridge Journal of Economics*, forthcoming.

R. Levine and D. Renelt (1992), A Sensitivity Analysis of Cross-Country Growth Regressions, *American Economic Review*, September.

A. Lewis (1954), Economic Development with Unlimited Supplies of Labour, *Manchester School*, May.

J. Lopez and A. Cruz (2000), 'Thirlwall's Law' and Beyond: the Latin American Experience, *Journal of Post Keynesian Economics*, Spring

R. Lucas (1988), On the Mechanics of Economic Development, *Journal of Monetary Economics*, vol. 22.

J. McCombie (1985a), Increasing Returns and the Manufacturing Industries: Some Empirical Issues, *Manchester School*, March.

J. McCombie (1985b), Economic Growth, the Harrod Foreign Trade Multiplier and the Hicks Super Multiplier, *Applied Economics*, February.

J. McCombie and J.R. de Ridder (1983), Increasing Returns, Productivity and Output Growth: The Case of the United States, *Journal of Post Keynesian Economics*, Spring.

J. McCombie and A.P. Thirlwall (1994), *Economic Growth and the Balance of Payments Constraint* (London: Macmillan).

J. McCombie and A.P. Thirlwall (1997), The Dynamic Harrod Foreign Trade Multiplier and the Demand Oriented Approach to Economic Growth: An Evaluation, *International Review of Applied Economics*, January.

A. Maddison (1970), *Economic Progress and Policy in Developing Countries* (London: Allen & Unwin).

T. Malthus (1798), *Essay on the Principle of Population* (London: Penguin, 1983).

K. Marx (1867), *Capital: A Critique of Political Economy, Vol. 1* (reprinted New York: International Publishers, 1967).

T.R. Michl (1985), International Comparisons of Productivity Growth: Verdoorn's Law Revisited, *Journal of Post Keynesian Economics*, Summer

J.C. Moreno-Brid (1998), Balance of Payments Constrained Economic Growth: The Case of Mexico, *Banca Nazionale del Lavoro Quarterly Review*, December.

J.C. Moreno-Brid (1999), Mexico's Economic Growth and the Balance of Payments Constraint: A Cointegration Analysis, *International Review of Applied Economics* vol. 13, no. 2.

G. Myrdal (1957), *Economic Theory and Underdeveloped Regions* (London: Duckworth).

R. Nelson (1956), A Theory of the Low Level Equilibrium Trap in Underdeveloped Countries, *American Economic Review*, December.

M. Nureldin-Hussain (1999), The Balance of Payments Constraint and Growth Rate Differences among African and East Asian Economies, *African Development Review*, June.

A. Okun (1962), Potential GNP: Its Measurement and Significance, *Proceedings of the Business and Finance Statistics Section of the American Statistical Association*.

R. Prebisch (1950), *The Economic Development of Latin America and its Principal Problems* (New York: ECLA, UN Dept. of Economic Affairs).

D. Ricardo (1817), *Principles of Political Economy and Taxation* (reprinted London: Everyman, 1992).

J. Robinson (1956), *The Accumulation of Capital* (London: Macmillan).

P. Romer (1986), Increasing Returns and Long Run Growth, *Journal of Political Economy*, October.

R. Sandilands (1990), Nicholas Kaldor's Notes on Allyn Young's LSE Lectures, 1927–29, *Journal of Economic Studies*, vol. 17, no. 3/4.

A. Santos-Paulino and A.P. Thirlwall (2001), The Impact of Trade Liberalisation on Export Growth, Import Growth, the Balance of Trade and the Balance of Payments of Developing Countries, University of Kent, mimeo.

T.W. Schultz (1961), Investment in Human Capital, *American Economic Review*, March.

D. Seers (1962), A Model of Comparative Rates of Growth of the World Economy, *Economic Journal*, March.

A. Smith (1776), *An Inquiry into the Nature and Causes of the Wealth of Nations* (London: Straham and Caddell).

R. Solow (1956), A Contribution to the Theory of Economic Growth, *Quarterly Journal of Economics*, February.

R. Solow (1957), Technical Change and the Aggregate Production Function, *Review of Economics and Statistics*, August.

R. Summers and A. Heston (1991), The Penn World Table (Mark 5): An Expanded Set of International Comparisons 1950–1966, *Quarterly Journal of Economics*, May.

F. Targetti and A.P. Thirlwall (1989), *The Essential Kaldor* (London: Duckworth).

A.P. Thirlwall (1969), Okun's Law and the Natural Rate of Growth, *Southern Economic Journal*, July.

A.P. Thirlwall (1979), The Balance of Payments Constraint as an Explanation of International

Growth Rate Differences, *Banca Nazionale del Lavoro Quarterly Review*, March.

A.P. Thirlwall (1983), Foreign Trade Elasticities in Centre–Periphery Models of Growth and Development, *Banca Nazionale del Lavoro Quarterly Review*, September.

A.P. Thirlwall (1986), A General Model of Growth and Development on Kaldorian Lines, *Oxford Economic Papers*, July.

A.P. Thirlwall (1987a), *Nicholas Kaldor* (Brighton: Harvester Wheatsheaf).

A.P. Thirlwall (1987b), *Keynes and Economic Development* (London: Macmillan).

A.P. Thirlwall (1999), *Growth and Development: with Special Reference to Developing Economies*, 6th edn (London: Macmillan).

A.P. Thirlwall (2000), Trade Agreements, Trade Liberalisation and Economic Growth: A Selective Survey, *African Development Review*, December.

A.P. Thirlwall and G. Sanna (1996), '"New" Growth Theory and the Macrodeterminants of Growth: An Evaluation and Further Evidence', in P. Arestis (ed.), *Employment, Economic Growth and the Tyranny of the Market: Essays in Honour of Paul Davidson, Vol. 2* (Cheltenham, UK and Brookfield, US: Edward Elgar).

UNCTAD (1999), *Trade and Development Report* (Geneva: UNCTAD).

P.J. Verdoorn (1949), Fattori che Regolano lo Sviluppo della Produttivita del Lavoro, *L'Industria*, no. 1. English translation by A.P. Thirlwall in L. Pasinetti (ed.), *Italian Economic*

Papers Vol. II (Oxford: Oxford University Press, 1993).

World Bank (1991), *World Development Report* (Washington: World Bank).

Allyn Young (1928), Increasing Returns and Economic Progress, *Economic Journal*, December.

Alwyn Young (1995), The Tyranny of Numbers: Confronting the Statistical Realities of the East Asian Growth Experience, *Quarterly Journal of Economics*, August.

Index